GREEN LANTERN

WANTED: HAL JORDAN

Green Lantern
Wanted: Hal Jordan

Geoff Johns Writer

Wanted: Hal Jordan
Ivan Reis Penciller
Oclair Albert Inker
Moose Baumann Colorist

Mystery of the Star Sapphire
Daniel Acuña Art and color

Rob Leigh/Travis Lanham Letterers

Cover illustration by Ethan Van Sciver
Cover color by Moose Baumann
Logo by Daniel Gelon

GREEN LANTERN- WANTED: HAL JORDAN

Published by DC Comics.

DC Comics
1700 Broadway
New York, NY 10019
A Warner Bros. Entertainment Company
Printed in Canada.
First Printing.

Hardcover ISBN: 1-4012-1339-1
Hardcover ISBN: 978-1-4012-1339-8
Softcover ISBN: 1-4012-1590-4
Softcover ISBN: 978-1-4012-1590-3

**"In brightest day, in blackest night,
no evil shall escape my sight!
Let those who worship evil's might
Beware my power, Green Lantern's light!"**

—The oath of the Green Lanterns

PREVIOUSLY IN **GREEN LANTERN...**

Hal Jordan had been the greatest officer of the Green Lantern Corps, an intergalactic peacekeeping force armed with the ultimate weapon — a ring limited only by willpower. But Jordan became possessed and driven mad by the evil entity Parallax, and when his hometown of Coast City was destroyed, he decimated the Green Lantern Corps in a desperate attempt to rebuild the city and was himself killed by his comrades.

Years later, however, Jordan was resurrected and freed of the Parallax entity. It was revealed that Sinestro, the rogue Green Lantern, had conspired with Parallax to destroy Jordan. But with the final defeat of Parallax, Sinestro was once again exiled to the antimatter universe.

Jordan returned to active duty with the newly re-formed Green Lantern Corps. Because of the new structure of the Corps, Jordan now has a partner in patrolling galactic sector 2814 — John Stewart, himself a veteran Green Lantern.

Jordan also set about restoring his civilian life, moving to the reconstructed Coast City and reenlisting in the Air Force.

But his peaceful new existence was short-lived. First, Earth's heroes fought in a crisis that threatened to wipe out all reality, and in its wake, distrust of superheroes accelerated worldwide, leading several countries to sign a Freedom of Power Treaty which prohibited foreign superheroes from acting within participating nations.

Not long afterward, Jordan and Stewart, in pursuit of the super-villain Evil Star, passed into Chinese airspace in violation of the treaty. The Lanterns tried to explain that their duties as protectors of the sector superseded any terrestrial laws, but China's national super-team, the Great Ten, and Russia's armored Rocket Red Brigade intercepted them.

After that incident, the Air Force sent Jordan on a bombing run against terrorist camps in the former Soviet Union. While flying without his ring, Jordan and two of his fellow pilots — Shane "Rocket-Man" Sellers and Jillian "Cowgirl" Pearlman — were shot down and held in a terrorist POW camp for months. The three pilots were eventually rescued...

...and now the story continues...

Green Lantern #14
Cover art by **Ethan Van Sciver**

WANTED: HAL JORDAN
Chapter One

HAL JORDAN.
YOU HAVE BEEN CHOSEN.
ALTHOUGH I HEARD ABIN SUR'S VOICE, IT WAS HIS POWER RING TALKING.
IT WAS THE RING'S ENERGY THAT SURROUNDED ME.
IT WAS THE RING THAT FLEW ME ACROSS THE CALIFORNIA DESERT.
TO THE DYING ALIEN.
HE'S GOING TO ASK ME IF I ACCEPT THIS DUTY.
HAL JORDAN OF EARTH.
I REACH OUT FOR THE RING.
BUT SOMETHING'S DIFFERENT.

THIS RING DOES NOT BELONG TO YOU!

THIS IS WRONG.
ABIN SUR HAD A SOFT SMILE ON HIS FACE WHEN HE DIED. HE LAUGHED TO HIMSELF AS HE HANDED ME HIS POWER RING.
"AN EARTHMAN..." HE MUTTERED. "I NEVER THOUGHT I'D LIVE TO SEE THE DAY."
ABIN SUR MADE A JOKE IN THE FACE OF DEATH.
HE'S NOT JOKING NOW.
YOU ARE NOT WORTHY OF BEING AN OFFICER OF THE GREEN LANTERN CORPS.
YOU ABANDONED THE RING WHEN YOU AND YOUR FRIENDS NEEDED IT MOST.
THINGS CHANGE IN FRONT OF ME. FROM YEARS AGO TO MONTHS.
I'M BACK IN MY F-22 OVER CHECHNYA.
WE WERE TARGETING A TERRORIST GROUP RESPONSIBLE FOR AN ATTACK ON A U.S. BATTLESHIP THAT KILLED 72 NAVY SAILORS.
I LEFT MY POWER RING BACK AT EDWARDS. IT SAT IN MY LOCKER WITH ITS BATTERY.
I NEVER WEAR THE RING WHEN I FLY.

I WAS SHOT DOWN, ALONG WITH COWGIRL AND ROCKET-MAN.
KRAK
I DIDN'T HAVE THE RING TO TRANSLATE THE TERRORISTS' THREATS BUT THE INFLECTION IN THEIR VOICES TOLD ME EVERYTHING I NEEDED TO KNOW.
I BECAME A PRISONER OF WAR.
I TRIED TO SUMMON THE RING FOR TWO DAYS. THE CHARGE WAS TOO LOW.
FOR FOURTEEN WEEKS I NEVER SAW COWGIRL OR ROCKET-MAN. I DIDN'T KNOW IF THEY WERE DEAD OR ALIVE.
THEY DRAGGED ME INTO AN INTERROGATION ROOM EVERY NIGHT FOR THE FIRST TWO MONTHS.
I DIDN'T TELL THEM ANYTHING BUT MY NAME, RANK, SERIAL NUMBER AND DATE OF BIRTH.
THEY DIDN'T LIKE THAT VERY MUCH.
I SPENT THE REST OF MY TIME PLANNING AN ESCAPE. WEARING DOWN A LINK IN THE CHAINS AROUND MY WRISTS.
AND REMEMBERING SOMETHING JOHN MCCAIN SAID--
--"WE ARE TAUGHT TO UNDERSTAND, CORRECTLY, THAT COURAGE IS NOT THE ABSENCE OF FEAR, BUT THE CAPACITY FOR ACTION DESPITE OUR FEARS."
I FIGURED I WAS TWO DAYS AWAY FROM BREAKING A LINK WHEN I HEARD ROCKET-MAN'S SCREAMS ECHO IN THE HALLS. I LATER LEARNED HE'D BROKEN HIS LEG IN THE CRASH.
LIKE ME, ROCKET-MAN REFUSED TO REVEAL ANYTHING TO OUR CAPTORS.
AS SOON AS HIS LEG HAD STARTED TO HEAL, THOSE MONSTERS BROKE IT AGAIN.
AND THEN I SAW HER.

COWGIRL.
SHE WAS FIGHTING THEM AS THEY DRAGGED HER TOWARD THE SCREAMS. CURSING THEM. CALLING THEM NAMES.
SPITTING IN THEIR FACES.
I REACHED THROUGH THE BARS AS SHE PASSED.
I TOUCHED HER HAND.
OUR EYES MET.
I'M SO SORRY.

I DIDN'T KNOW HIS NAME, BUT HE WAS OBVIOUSLY THE ONE IN CHARGE. I CALLED HIM BONES--
KRAKK
AARGHH!
--BECAUSE HE SEEMED TO ENJOY BREAKING THEM.
MONTHS OF FUN AND YET YOU STILL REMAIN SILENT.
YOU HAVE REFUSED TO TELL US WHAT WE WANT TO KNOW ABOUT THE WEAKNESSES THAT CAN BE EXPLOITED WITHIN THE AMERICAN AIR FORCE.
WE ONLY ASK FOR SIMPLE WORDS TO RELIEVE YOU OF YOUR PAIN.
WHEN I BREAK HER...
HAL!
...YOU WILL BREAK.
I HEARD COWGIRL STRUGGLE.
I HEARD THEM HIT HER.
AGAIN AND AGAIN.
CHNKK
BROKE.

I GRABBED BONES' FACE.
HIS SMILE DISAPPEARED UNDER MY BROKEN FINGERS.
BLAM
I SLAMMED HIS HEAD AGAINST THE WALL.
AGAIN.
AND AGAIN.
HE SAID WE WERE AT WAR.
AND AT THIS MOMENT WE WERE.
UNN!
BLAMM

AS THE GUNSHOT ECHOED THROUGH THE HALLS, WE KNEW IT WOULDN'T BE LONG BEFORE MORE OF THEM SHOWED.
IF WE STOPPED MOVING WE PROBABLY WOULDN'T GET OUT ALIVE.
BUT WE HAD TO.
ALL OF US.
BLAMM BLAMM
SOMEHOW WE MADE OUR WAY OUTSIDE. A BLIZZARD MASKED OUR TRAIL.
WE SPENT TWO DAYS MOVING THROUGH THE FOREST. UNTIL ONE NIGHT WE SAW A LIGHT.
IT WAS A FIRE. STARTED BY A GROUP OF MOUNTAIN CLIMBERS. THEY TOOK US IN.
I SPENT A WEEK IN THE HOSPITAL ON RHEIN-MAIN AIR FORCE BASE IN GERMANY. ANOTHER ONE AT EDWARDS.
WHEN AN AIR TEAM FINALLY LOCATED THE CAMP, IT HAD BEEN DESERTED. BONES AND HIS GUNMEN HAD MOVED ON.
WE'RE STILL TRYING TO.
THE LEAGUE WASN'T AROUND TO LOOK FOR ME. THEY THOUGHT I FLEW OFF TO SPACE ON ANOTHER CORPS MISSION.
WHEN THEY FINALLY FOUND OUT, EVERY ONE OF THEM CAME TO ME. I DIDN'T ASK FOR THEIR APOLOGIES BUT I GOT THEM. FROM EVERYONE BUT OLLIE.
OLLIE SAID WHAT I SAID TO MYSELF A HUNDRED TIMES A NIGHT IN THAT CELL--

"--YOU SHOULD'VE KEPT THE RING ON."
WHO MISSED THEIR APPOINTMENTS?
DON'T ACT SURPRISED, GENERAL STONE. ALL OF THEM.
COLONEL SHANE "ROCKET-MAN" SELLERS. CAPTAIN JILLIAN "COWGIRL" PEARLMAN. AND CAPTAIN HAL "HIGHBALL" JORDAN.
THESE FORMER P.O.W.S ARE BACK ON ACTIVE DUTY PROVIDED THEY ATTEND MANDATORY THERAPY SESSIONS--
COWGIRL'S ALREADY PROACTIVE--
WHICH I WARNED HER AGAINST. NOW WHERE ARE THEY?!
THIS IS OUR KIND OF THERAPY.
TALKING WITH PEOPLE WHO HAVE BEEN WHERE YOU'VE BEEN, INSTEAD OF PEOPLE WHO WANT TO SLAP A LABEL ON YOUR PROBLEM AND PRESCRIBE YOU A PILL.
MBB
THIS IS MY LAST ROUND, GUYS. GOTTA GET HOME. OLDEST HAD BASEBALL TRYOUTS TODAY.
YOU GO ON AHEAD, ROCKET-MAN. BEER'S ON ME TONIGHT.
ROCKET-MAN PROMISED HIS KIDS HE'D BE AN ASTRONAUT ONE DAY. HE TOLD THEM THAT'S WHERE HE WAS ALL THOSE MONTHS. UP ON THE MOON.
NOW HIS KIDS BEG HIM TO TAKE THEM THERE EVERY NIGHT. HURTS MORE THAN HIS LEG, I'D GUESS.
COWGIRL SEEMS A FEW STEPS AHEAD OF ROCKET-MAN AND ME. SHE'S BEEN SMILING ALL DAY DESPITE US GOING DOWN MEMORY LANE.
YOU ASK ME, BOYS, THIS IS ALL BEHIND US.
I WANT TO TELL THEM, BUT SOMETHING KEEPS STOPPING ME. I'M SUPPOSED TO HAVE A "SECRET IDENTITY," RIGHT? IT'S TO PROTECT THEM...NOT ME...
...I SHOULD'VE KEPT THE RING O

TWENTY-FOUR HOURS LATER MY WORLD TURNS UPSIDE DOWN AGAIN.
COWGIRL SAID SHE TOLD YOU AT PANCHO'S.
TOLD US WHAT? THAT YOU OUND THESE BASTARDS? THAT YOU WERE SENDING HER ON A MISSION TO FINALLY SHUT THEM DOWN?
SHE DIDN'T TELL US ANYTHING, GENERAL.
WHEN DID IT HAPPEN?
SUGARSNAP AND WHIMS MADE THE RUN WITH HER. COWGIRL GOT HIT. WE LOST CONTACT WITH HER TEN MINUTES AGO.
IT'S GOING TO TAKE A RESCUE TEAM TOO LONG TO GET THERE. BONES AND HIS CREW WORK FAST. IF SHE SURVIVED--
--THEY PROBABLY ALREADY HAVE HER.
I HAVE TO GO.
GO? GO WHERE, HIGHBALL?
I LEAVE IT TO GENERAL STONE TO MAKE UP AN EXCUSE.
IT'S TIME TO CLOCK IN.
HE'S THE ONLY ONE ON BASE WHO KNOWS WHAT MY OTHER JOB IS.
IN BRIGHTEST DAY, IN BLACKEST NIGHT--
--NO EVIL SHALL ESCAPE MY SIGHT--
--LET THOSE WHO WORSHIP EVIL'S MIGHT--
--BEWARE MY POWER--

--GREEN LANTERN'S LIGHT!

MOSCOW, RUSSIA.
CENTRAL COMMAND CENTER OF THE ROCKET RED BRIGADE.
<NUMBER NINE. THE FREEDOM OF POWER TREATY HAS BEEN BREACHED. SATELLITES HAVE REGISTERED AN UNIDENTIFIED FLYING BEING WITHIN OUR BORDERS.>
<LOCK AND VISUALIZE U.F.B.>
<IT'S THE AMERICAN. AGAIN.>
<CONTACT NUMBER ONE.>
<TELL HIM WE FINALLY HAVE GREEN LANTERN IN OUR SIGHTS.>
THE WRECKAGE IS RIGHT WHERE THEY SAID IT WAS. JET'S BEEN STRIPPED OF ITS AIM-120C AIR-TO-AIR MISSILES AND ITS PILOT.
SNOW EVENTUALLY COVERS ANY TRAIL OUT HERE.
EVENTUALLY.
BUT NOT YET.

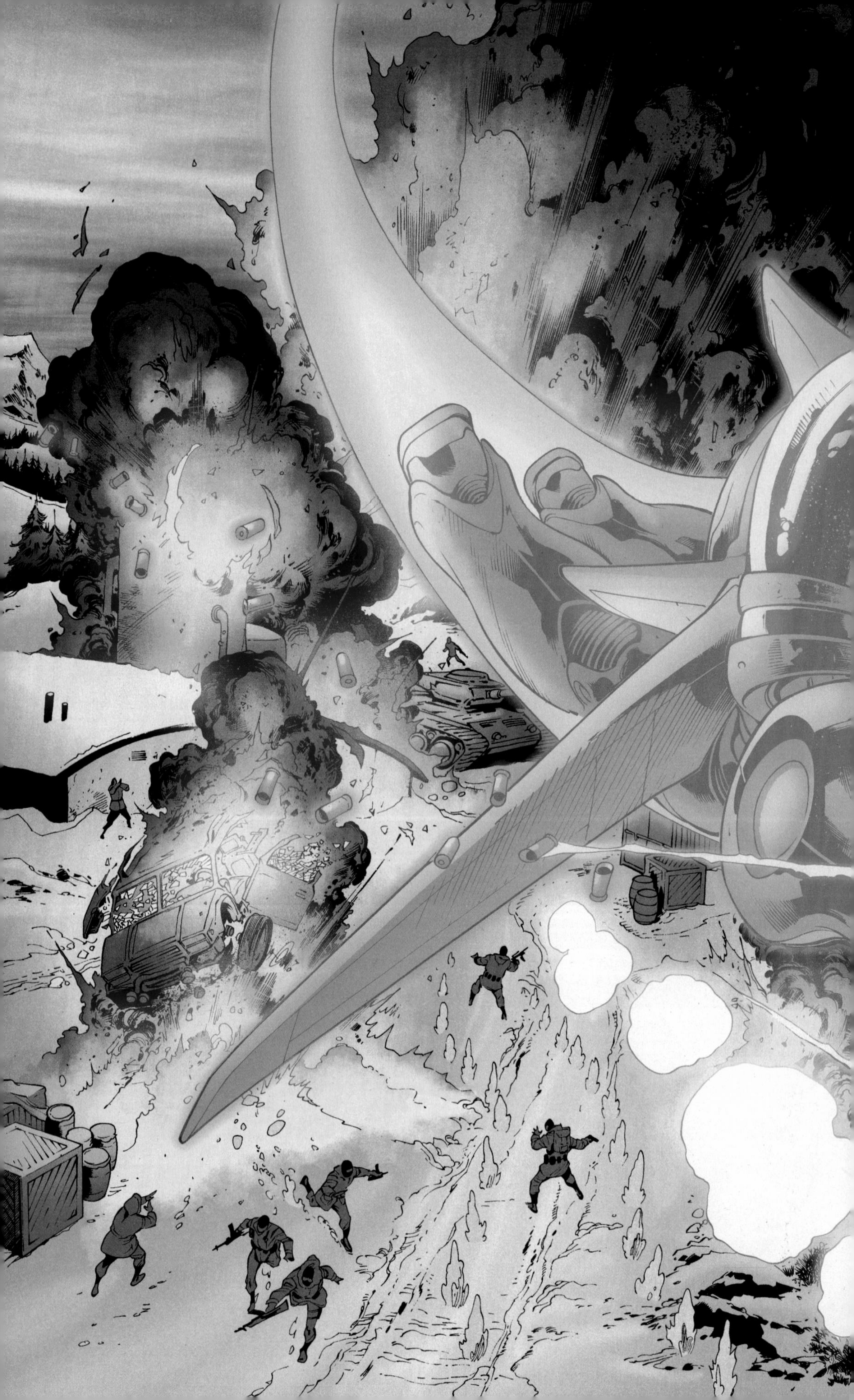

I RECOGNIZE MOST OF THEM BY THEIR VOICES.
BUT THIS TIME MY RING IS TRANSLATING. I CAN UNDERSTAND THEM. THIS TIME THEY'RE SCARED.
THEY SHOULD BE.
THE RING IS PROGRAMMED TO DO EVERYTHING I COMMAND IT TO DO EXCEPT KILL.
THE GREEN LANTERN CORPS HAS A CODE AGAINST LETHAL FORCE.
BUT THESE SCUM DON'T KNOW THAT.
BOOM
BEING HERE WITH THE RING ON...WHAT TOOK ME MONTHS TO OPEN NOW TAKES ME SECONDS.
SKANG
SKANG
SKANG
I WON'T LET COWGIRL SPEND ANOTHER SECOND HERE.

RING.
SCAN THE BUILDING. LOCATE CAPTAIN JILLIAN PEARLMAN.
SCANNING.
HAL!
WHEN I BREAK HER...
...YOU WILL BREAK.
CAPTAIN JILLIAN PEARLMAN NOT FOUND WITHIN IMMEDIATE PREMISES.
BLAM
FORCE FIELD MELTS THE BULLET INTO SLAG.
THE REVERB STINGS MY EARS.

I STING BACK.
WHOOM
AARRH!
WHERE IS SHE, DAMMIT?!
TALK, BONES!
‹YOU?›
‹I KNOW YOU.›
TRANSLATING: "YOU? ...I KNOW YOU."
WHERE IS SHE?!

<I TOLD YOU. WHEN SHE BREAKS...>
"I TOLD YOU. WHEN SHE BREAKS..."
<...SO WILL YOU.>
"...SO WILL YOU."
FZZAK
AARRH!
FZZAK
AAIEEEE!

THE GLOBAL GUARDIANS?
WHAT THE HELL DID YOU JUST DO?!?
IT'S NOT WHAT WE DID, GREEN LANTERN.
IT'S WHAT YOU DID.
GLOBAL GUARDIANS TO UNITED NATIONS. WE HAVE A SITUATION IN NORTHERN CHECHNYA.
GREEN LANTERN HAS JUST MURDERED TWO DOZEN PRISONERS WE WERE ABOUT TO TAKE INTO CUSTODY.
PERMISSION TO BRING WAR CRIME CHARGES AGAINST HIM.

PERMISSION GRANTED.
SHRRIP
⟨APPROACH GREEN LANTERN WITH CAUTION. WEAPON SYSTEMS ON HIGH.⟩
I'M ON HIS TRAIL.
TELL YOUR BENEFACTOR I'LL HAVE THE GREEN LANTERN ON ICE WITHIN THE HOUR.
YOU'LL HAVE SOME COMPETITION, HUNGER DOG.
THE FACELESS HUNTERS AND THE DOMINATOR JUST TOLD ME THE SAME THING. MAY THE BEST TRACKER WIN.
LORAGG OUT.
SIR. THE PRICE ON GREEN LANTERN'S HEAD HAS BEEN DOUBLED. THE THAMES RIVER BAR HAS EMPTIED OUT IN PURSUIT OF THE CORPS OFFICER.
HE WILL BE IN OUR CUSTODY BEFORE ANY OTHER. DEAD OR ALIVE.
DEAD OR ALIVE? I TOLD YOU I WANT HIM ALIVE, LORAGG.
I WANT HAL JORDAN DISGRACED AND PROVEN AS UNWORTHY AS I KNOW HIM TO BE.

AND THEN I WANT MY FATHER'S RING BACK.

Green Lantern #15
Cover art by **Ethan Van Sciver**

WANTED: HAL JORDAN
Chapter Two

SPACE SECTOR 3601.
HANK HENSHAW.
KZZAT
ALSO KNOWN AS THE "CYBORG-SUPERMAN" AND HIGHMASTER OF THE MURDERING MANHUNTERS.
YOUR PRESENCE IS REQUESTED BY THE GUARDIANS OF THE UNIVERSE.
YOU WILL TELL US EVERYTHING YOU HAVE LEARNED WITHIN SPACE SECTOR 3601.
AND WHAT YOU KNOW ABOUT THE 52.

THE MONSTER THROWING ME THROUGH THE TREE CALLS HIMSELF THE *TASMANIAN DEVIL.*
HE WAS A MEMBER OF THE JUSTICE LEAGUE THE *LAST* TIM
I WAS ON THE TEAM. POWER GIR
SAID HE HAD A *CRUSH* ON ME.

WALLY AND RALPH NEVER LET ME HEAR THE END OF IT.
A FEW MONTHS AGO, THE TASMANIAN DEVIL RESURFACED AND JOINED UP WITH THE NEW GLOBAL GUARDIANS.
HIS NEW TEAM WANTS TO PROVE TO THE WORLD THAT PEOPLE LIKE US CAN ACT RESPONSIBLY WITHOUT GOVERNMENT RESTRICTIONS LIKE THE FREEDOM OF POWER TREATY.
IT'S A LAW THAT PROHIBITS FOREIGN METAHUMAN ACTIVITY WITHIN CERTAIN COUNTRIES.
I'VE VIOLATED IT SIX TIMES.
TODAY MAKES SEVEN.

AN HOUR AGO, ONE OF MY FRIENDS FROM EDWARDS--CAPTAIN JILLIAN "COWGIRL" PEARLMAN--WAS SHOT DOWN AND DRAGGED AWAY BY A GROUP OF CHECHNYA TERRORISTS.
I TOLD YOU BEFORE, TAZ.
YOU'RE NOT MY TYPE.
I TORE OPEN THEIR CAMP. THERE WAS NO SIGN OF HER.
BEFORE I HAD A CHANCE TO INTERROGATE HER CAPTORS--
--THE GLOBAL GUARDIANS BURNED THE FLESH OFF THEIR BONES.
WE'RE BRINGING YOU IN FOR THE MURDER OF TWENTY-THREE UNARMED WAR CRIMINALS, GREEN LANTERN.
YOU'RE THE ONE WHO KILLED THEM, JET, NOT ME.
WE DID IT TO SHOW THE WORLD WHAT YOU REALLY ARE, LANTERN. A BULLY LIKE YOUR HOMELAND.
BOOOOM
GLOSS HAS BEEN A FORCE OF GOOD IN CHINA FOR YEARS.
AND ANIMAL MAN PERSONALLY RECOMMENDED SOUTH AFRICA'S FREEDOM BEAST FOR LEAGUE MEMBERSHIP WHEN HE LEFT THE TEAM.
YOU DO NOT DESERVE THE HONOR OF BEING A MEMBER OF THE CORPS!
WHY ARE THEY ACTING LIKE THIS?
WHY FIGHT, GREEN LANTERN?

SHE'S STUNNING...
WHEN WE CAN LOVE.
COME HERE, MON AMI BEL.
A WAVE OF PHEROMONES HITS ME HARDER THAN A TWELVE-PACK. THE NEW CRIMSON FOX SHARES THE POWERS OF HER PREDECESSORS.

WHO ARE YOU?
I AM THE NEW HEIR TO THE D'ARAMIS COSMETICS FORTUNE.
I AM THE PASSION OF FRANCE.
JE SUIS LA CRAMOISI ROUUSE.
BUT SHE'S NOT COWGIRL.
RRRRRRFF!
I HAVE TO FIND COWGIRL.
FWAM
NN.
THE MORE YOU STRUGGLE, THE TIGHTER THE MANTICORE WILL SQUEEZE.
RRARRH!
YOU WILL HAND OVER WHAT HE WANTS, HAL JORDAN.
YOU WILL GIVE YOUR RING TO US--
--OR YOU WILL DIE.
HALT, HUMANS.
YOU HAVE SERVED YOUR PURPOSE THUS FAR, BUT DO NOT EXCEED OUR ORDERS.

I FEEL THEM RESISTING OUR COMMANDS, CHUN YULL. ESPECIALLY THE SYRIAN-- SANDSTORM.
I HEAR VOICES IN MY HEAD LIKE A FAINT ECHO.
RING. SCAN FOR TELEPATHS.
SCANNING.
OUR COMBINED MIND-POWERS STOLEN FROM THE MOON OF TITAN WILL CONTAIN THEIR FREE WILL LONG ENOUGH.
AFTER ALL, GORR NUM, THE GLOBAL GUARDIANS ARE NO GREEN LANTERNS.
I TOLD YOU WE WOULD BEAT HUNGER DOG TO THE PREY ONCE WE SCRAMBLED HIS POWER RING GEIGER.
HUNGER DOG'S HALFWAY AROUND THIS MUDBALL CHASING A FALSE SIGNAL. THE PRICE ON HAL JORDAN'S HEAD IS OURS.
TWO TELEPATHS DETECTED. FREQUENCY CORRELATES TO SATURN'S SUBATOMIC RACE OF KLARMARIANS.
MORE COMMONLY KNOWN THROUGHOUT THE UNIVERSE AS THE FACELESS HUNTERS.
WHERE ARE THEY?
THEY ARE CURRENTLY BASED ON THE THIRD NEUTRON OF AN ATOM WITHIN A SNOWFLAKE DIRECTLY IN FRONT OF US.
KRKKZZZ
FIRE!
OUR NEURON-NET HAS TEMPORARILY SHORT-CIRCUITED HIS POWER RING AND BRAIN.

IT IS TIME TO COLLECT OUR BOUNTY.

SOUTHERN CALIFORNIA.
AMON SUR?
YES, LORAGG?
I HAVE EXCELLENT NEWS. THE FACELESS HUNTERS OF SATURN HAVE CAPTURED THE GREEN LANTERN.
GIVE THEM OUR LOCATION. HAVE THEM BRING HIM TO ME.
THERE IS A PROBLEM, AMON. THE HUNTERS HAVE BEEN UNABLE TO REMOVE THE GREEN LANTERN'S POWER RING FROM HIS HAND.
PERHAPS IF THEY DISMEMBERED HIM--
IF HAL JORDAN DIES MY FATHER'S RING IS PROGRAMMED TO FOLLOW CORPS CODE AND SEEK OUT THE CLOSEST REPLACEMENT FOR OUR SECTOR.
BUT SURELY THAT REPLACEMENT WOULD BE YOU.
IF I AM IN THE VICINITY WHEN HAL JORDAN IS KILLED--
--IT WILL BE.

SALISBURY, ENGLAND.
MY ROOMMATE SAYS ALIENS HELPED THE DRUIDS BUILD STONEHENGE. THE SAME ONES THAT CARVED THE FACES ON EASTER ISLAND.
YOU DON'T REALLY BELIEVE THAT, DO YOU?
I BELIEVE IN A LOT OF THINGS, KRYSTAL.
LIKE LOVE AT FIRST SIGHT.
WHEN I SAW YOU AT THE HOSTEL, I KNEW WE WERE MEANT FOR EACH OTHER.
CHRIS, NOT YET, OKAY? W JUST MET.
DO YOU BELIEVE IN LOVE AT FIRST SIGHT?
HE LIES.
DID YOU HEAR THAT?
HEAR WHAT?
IT WAS A WOMAN'S VOICE.
HE DOES NOT LOVE YOU.
THERE IT IS AGAIN.
I DIDN'T HEAR ANYTHING.
I LOVE YOU.

SHRRAKK
AAIEEEE!!
KRRKKLL
KRYSTAL?!
YOU ARE A WEAK MALE SPECIMEN.
SNKKRZZZ
THIS FEMALE HOST IS NOT THE BODY MY CHOSEN EARTH-MATE DESIRES.
I MUST FIND THE BODY THAT IS.

‹SHE'S *PRETTY*.›
‹AS *PRETTY* AS SHE WAS THE *LAST* TIME WE FOUND HER.›
I DON'T KNOW WHAT Y'ALL SAID, BUT I'M BETTIN' IT WASN'T NOTHIN' *NICE!*
YOU CAN DROP ME OFF HERE.
‹*STOP!*›
SKRAASSHH

<SHE LOOKS LIKE AN ANGEL, BUT SHE IS A DEVIL. BOMBING OUR CAMPS. KILLING OUR BROTHERS.>
<YES. SHE WAS LUCKY ALL WE DID WAS LOCK HER IN A CELL.>
<BUT THIS TIME, CAPTAIN PEARLMAN, FOR LEADING GREEN LANTERN TO OUR CAMP, WE WILL DO MUCH MORE THAN THAT.>
BLAM
BLAM BLAM BLAM
<AMERICAN WITCH!>
BLAM
BLAM

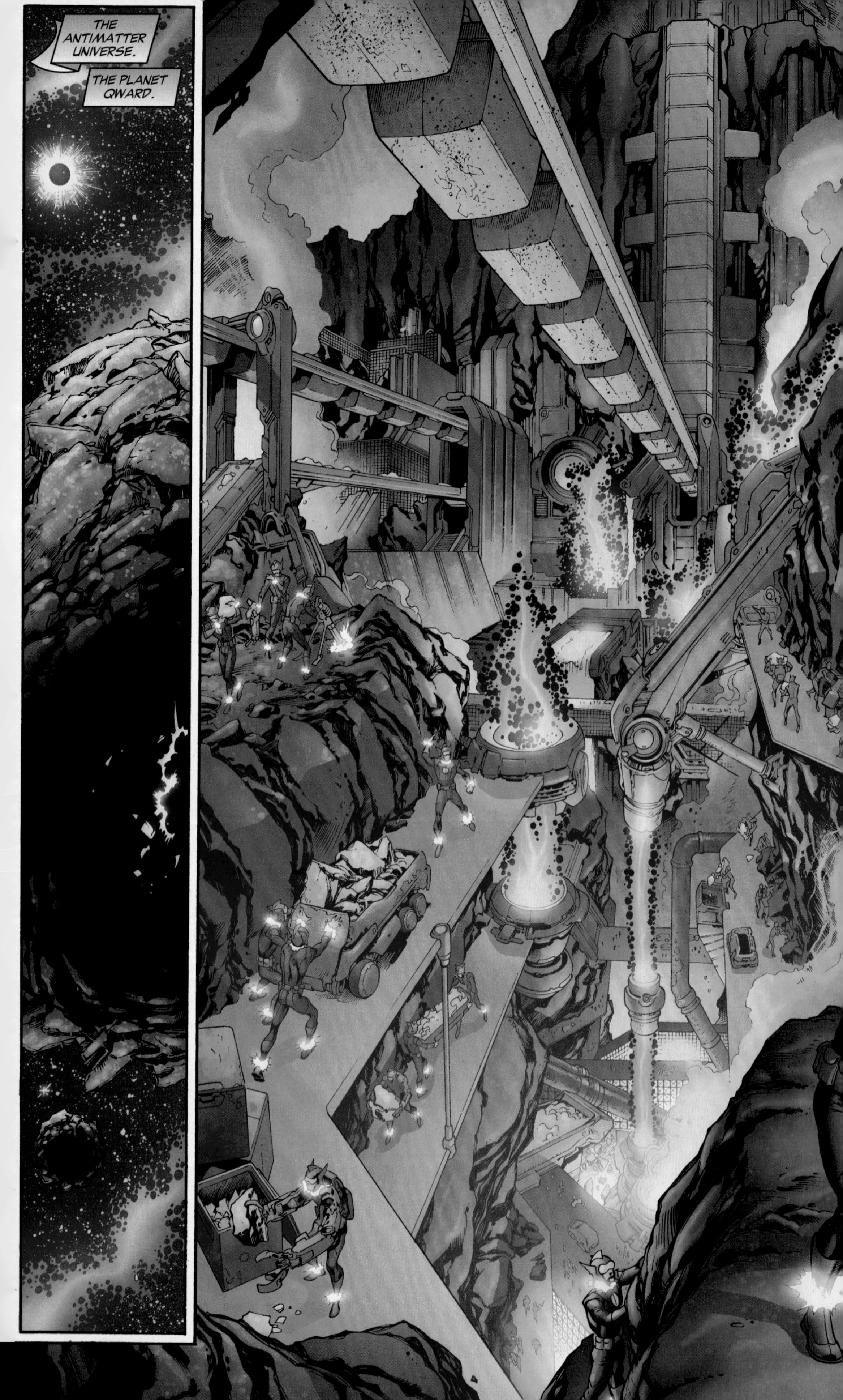

THE ANTIMATTER UNIVERSE.
THE PLANET QWARD.

THE WEAPONERS FORGED SINESTRO'S POWER RING WITHIN THIS CANYON.
OUR PEOPLE WERE THE ONES WHO GAVE SINESTRO HIS WEAPON TO COMBAT OUR OPPOSITE UNIVERSE AND ITS GUARDIANS WHO BANISHED HIM.
SINESTRO WAS NEVER OUR REPRESENTATIVE. HE IS OBSESSED WITH HIS OWN PHILOSOPHY OF ORDER.
HE REJECTED OURS, FABRIKANT.

WE MUST REVOLT BEFORE SINESTRO ACQUIRES THE HERALD. WE ARE STILL SINESTRO'S BETTERS. WE ARE HIS MASTERS!
WE ARE NOT HIS--
SLAVES.

IF YOU REFUSE TO WORK--
--YOU WILL BE MY LUNCH.
AAAIEE!
SKRUNCH

I NEED ROOKIES TO TRAIN.
INITIATE RING SPAWN.
ARKILLO-- SINESTRO CORPS OFFICER OF SECTOR 674 RECOGNIZED.

RING SPAWN SIX INITIATED.
SUBATOMIC POLARITY WITHIN POWER RINGS REVERSING. WORM-HOLE TO THE POSITIVE MATTER UNIVERSE BREACHED.
SCANNING SPACE SECTOR 45.
SCANNING SPACE SECTOR 1130.

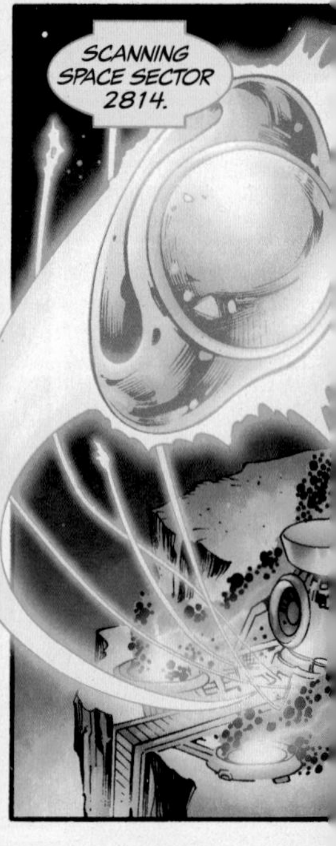
SCANNING SPACE SECTOR 2814.

CLOAKING OFF.
VUMMMMMMMMMMMMM
CAN YOU READ THE LANTERN'S STRUGGLING THOUGHTS, CHUN YULL? HE IS TRYING TO MOVE. HE MAY BREAK THE NEURON-NET.
Hhn. THEY WANT THE GREEN LANTERN ALIVE.
BUT THAT DOESN'T MEAN HE CAN'T BE A VEGETABLE.
WE'LL SIMPLY EMPTY HIS MIND AS WE DID THE GLOBAL GUARDIANS'--
FOR THE LAST TIME, GREEN LANTERN.
BOOM

BY THE AUTHORITY OF RUSSIA'S ROCKET RED BRIGADE--
YOU ARE UNDER ARREST.

ROCKET REDS? BELIEVE IT OR NOT--I'M HAPPY TO SEE YOU.
‹IT APPEARS THE AMERICAN IS NOT WORKING ALONE.›
‹PERHAPS HE PLANS FOR AN ALIEN INVASION OF OUR HOME-LAND.›
I'VE HELPED SAVE THIS PLANET A DOZEN TIMES FROM BEING INVADED. THESE GUYS WERE AFTER ME.
THEY WERE CONTROLLING THE GLOBAL GUARDIANS.
ACCORDING TO THE GLOBAL GUARDIANS' REPORTS TO THE UNITED NATIONS EARLIER TODAY--
--YOU MURDERED TWENTY-THREE SUSPECTED TERRORISTS THEY HAD TAKEN INTO CUSTODY. PERHAPS YOU ARE ATTEMPTING TO COVER THOSE UP WITH THEIR MURDERS.
THE GLOBAL GUARDIANS AREN'T DEAD. THEIR BRAINS JUST NEED A REBOOT.
EVERYONE AROUND THE WORLD KNOWS OF YOUR CRIMES, GREEN LANTERN. EVERYONE KNOWS YOU ARE GUILTY.
WHAT ELSE IS NEW?

KOOM
I'M GIVING YOU MY WORD, I'LL LEAVE RUSSIA AS SOON I'VE FOUND WHO I'M SEARCHING FOR.
YOU TRY TO ESCORT ME OUT NOW AND I'LL TEAR APART EVERY LAST ONE OF YOU.
BWOOSH
LNNN!
I'M SORRY, GREEN LANTERN--

--BUT THIS IS FOR YOUR OWN GOOD.
YOU'RE COMING HOME WITH US.
YOU MAY AS WELL INDUCT THE OLD GREEN LANTERN INTO YOUR JUSTICE LEAGUE.
THIS ONE IS OURS.

Green Lantern #16
Cover art by **Ethan Van Sciver**

WANTED: HAL JORDAN
Chapter Three

MY POWER RING WAS GIVEN TO ME BY A DYING ALIEN NAMED ABIN SUR.
IT GIVES ME THE ABILITIES TO FLY, GENERATE FORCE FIELDS, AND CREATE ANY OBJECT I CAN IMAGINE.
THAT'S WHY I NEVER WORE THE RING WHEN I FLEW MY JETS. I DIDN'T WANT A SAFETY NET.
AND I DIDN'T HAVE ONE WHEN MY F-22 WAS SHOT DOWN BY A GROUP OF TERRORISTS OVER RUSSIA.
FOR MONTHS, TWO OF MY FRIENDS AND I WERE HELD AS P.O.W.'S.
YESTERDAY, COWGIRL WENT ON ANOTHER RUN AGAINST THEM WITHOUT US. OVER-EAGER AND FLYING LOW, SHE WAS SHOT DOWN.
I TORE APART THE TERRORIST CAMP LOOKING FOR HER.
AND WHILE I'VE BEEN TRYING TO FIND HER, I'VE BEEN ATTACKED BY EXTRATERRESTRIAL BOUNTY HUNTERS OUT TO COLLECT A PRICE SOMEONE PUT ON MY HEAD.
NOW, BECAUSE KARMA'S STILL CHASING ME DOWN, I'VE GOT RUSSIA'S ARMORED WATCHDOGS ON MY ASS.
THE ROCKET REDS WANT TO ARREST ME FOR PATROLLING THE PLANET AND CROSSING THEIR BORDERS...

...BUT I DON'T THINK MY FRIENDS ARE GOING TO LET THEM.

CLARK USUALLY GIVES ME A NOD AND A SMILE BEFORE WE PLAY PUNCH-OUT-THE-BAD-GUYS.
HE DIDN'T THIS TIME.
WHICH MEANS SUPERMAN'S NOT HAPPY ABOUT THE BRUISING HE'S HANDING OUT.
I'M SORRY ABOUT THIS, GENTLEMEN.
WE'RE SIMPLY HERE TO ESCORT OUR TEAM MEMBER OUT OF YOUR JURISDICTION.
THERE IS NOTHING SIMPLE ABOUT THIS, SUPERMAN. GREEN LANTERN HAS BEEN WARNED ON SEVERAL OCCASIONS.
JUSTICE LEAGUE MEMBER OR NOT, HE WILL BE MADE AN EXAMPLE OF.
I HEAR A FEW OF THE ROCKET REDS CONFESS THE TRUTH TO DIANA AS HER LASSO SNATCHES THEM UP.
I HOPE SHE DOESN'T UNDERSTAND RUSSIAN.
YOU'RE LUCKY WE'RE HERE, LANTERN.
WHEN WE HEARD THAT YOU'D BEEN ACCUSED OF KILLING A GROUP OF TERRORISTS TAKEN INTO CUSTODY, WE HAD TO TAKE A VOTE ON YOUR INNOCENCE.
A VOTE?
EVER SINCE BRUCE SET HER UP WITH THAT SECRET IDENTITY, DIANA'S GROWN A SENSE OF HUMOR.
GOTCHA.
ALL THESE YEARS AND I NEVER THOUGHT OF WONDER WOMAN AS...CUTE.
I HEAR SOME BONES BREAK AS SHE SWINGS HER LASSO AGAIN. THEN I HEAR A GROWL.

'S VIXEN.
SABERTOOTH TIGER.
KRASSHH
THE GLOBAL GUARDIANS HAVE SEEN BETTER DAYS. SMOKE'S POURING OUT OF THEIR EARS.
YOU THINK THE ROCKET REDS DID THIS?
I'D PUT THE BLAME ON THE ALIENS LYING NEXT TO THEM.
LOOKS LIKE WE BETTER EVACUATE THE GUARDIANS TOO.
I HAVE THEM.
KRZZZT
LIGHTNING!
KLANG
BATARANG JUST *MAGNETIZED* ROCKET RED ONE'S *ARMOR*.
ALREADY AHEAD OF YOU, BATMAN.
TZZRRAT

KRAKOOM

JEFF TURNS ON THE JUICE.

ONE BIG ASS *ELECTROMAGNET* COMIN' *UP*.

ROCKET RED ONE IS GOING TO HAVE ONE HELLUVA HEADACHE.

AW, I WAS JUST STARTING TO HAVE FUN!

THE LEAGUE'S THINNING OUT THE BRIGADE'S RANKS.

I NEED TO MAKE AN *ESCAPE* ROUTE.
FWOOM

KRZZZZZ
YOU NEED TO LEARN TO WATCH YOUR BACK, FLYBOY.
OLLIE TOLD US YOU MIGHT BE LOOKING FOR SOME PAYBACK ON THE GUYS THAT HELD YOU PRISONER.
THEY'RE ALREADY DEAD, CANARY.
NOW, I'VE GOTTA RUN.
WAIT A SECOND, OLD MAN! I THOUGHT THIS WAS THE PART WHERE YOU EXPLAIN WHAT'S GOING ON!
LATER.
THE LEAGUE BROKE AT LEAST A DOZEN INTERNATIONAL LAWS COMING IN HERE TO HELP YOU.

YOU'LL EXPLAIN NOW.

EVEN THROUGH MY FORCE FIELD, I CAN FEEL THE HEAT FROM ALAN'S FIRE.
I CAN'T IGNORE HIM.
SCANNING.
SCANNING.
SCANNING.
I CREATE A HALF-DOZEN SEARCH PROBES TO SCAN THE SURROUNDING FORESTS FOR COWGIRL.
AND I TALK.
BECAUSE OF ME, ONE OF MY FRIENDS IS LOST DOWN THERE. SHE WOULDN'T BE IN THIS MESS IF I'D PLAYED IT SAFE.
YOU NEVER PLAY IT SAFE.
YOU'D THINK AFTER PARALLAX I WOULD'VE LEARNED TO.
WHAT ARE YOU TALKING ABOUT?
YOU DIDN'T SHOOT THOSE PLANES DOWN. YOU DIDN'T LOCK THOSE CELL DOORS, HAL.
BUT I COULD'VE STOPPED IT IF I'D HAD MY RING, ALAN.

I HAVE TO FIND THIS GIRL.
AND I HAVE TO FIND HER NOW.
I'VE HEARD THAT WORRY IN YOUR VOICE BEFORE-- WITH CAROL. AS SOON AS YOU TWO GOT SERIOUS, YOU HIT THE ROAD WITH OLIVER.
BUT YOU'RE NOT RUNNING AWAY THIS TIME.
TELL ME HOW WE CAN HELP.
GET BACK THERE. TAKE THE GLOBAL GUARDIANS TO MARTIAN MANHUNTER. THE FACELESS HUNTERS SCRAMBLED THEIR MINDS. J'ONN CAN SET THEM RIGHT.
PULL WHAT STRINGS YOU'VE GOT LEFT IN CHECKMATE TO CLEAR MY NAME WITH THE UNITED NATIONS--
--AND APOLOGIZE FOR ME.
THE REST OF THIS IS ON MY SHOULDERS. AND MY PARTNER'S GOING TO HELP ME CARRY THE LOAD.

EDWARDS AIR FORCE BASE.
ZZRRAK
WHAT THE HELL'S GOING ON, GENERAL?
KEEP BACK, ROCKET-MAN.
WHOEVER'S ATTACKING IS HEADING FOR HANGAR 44--
--GREEN LANTERN'S EXTRATERRESTRIAL BRIG!
ZZRRAAAKKK
44
ZZRAAKK
ZZRAK
YOU HAVE **STOLEN** FROM ME JUST AS YOUR GREEN LANTERN HAS.
44

WE'VE GOT A BREACH IN HANGAR 44! REPEAT--A BREACH IN HANGAR 44!
STAY WHERE YOU ARE!
BRATTABRATTA
I WILL GO WHERE I CHOOSE TO.
...AND HIS SHIP.

LIKE MY FATHER, I HAVE *NO FEAR.*

AMON SUR?! YOU'VE COME TO *FREE* ME!
FREE YOU, REG H'RR?
YES! MY CONTRACT WITH YOU--
HAS BEEN *VOIDED.* YOU PROMISED *DELIVERY* OF THE GREEN LANTERN. YOU FALTERED AND *HE* CAPTURED *YOU.*

THE FACELESS HUNTERS HAVE LOST HIM AS WELL.
BUT THERE ARE MANY OTHERS AFTER HIM. GREEN LANTERN WILL BE *MINE...*
...AS WILL MY FATHER'S *POWER RING...*

BLAMM
BLAMM
SKUNCH
UNN!
KRIKKRAKK
KRASSH
VZZAP
WHAT?!?
CAPTAIN JILLIAN "COWGIRL" PEARLMAN LOCATED.
‹DEATH TO AMERICA.›

KRAK
ARR!

IT TAKES EVERYTHING I HAVE TO STOP THE SOLDIERS I MADE FROM BREAKING EVERY BONE IN HIS BODY.
WE HAVE TO PLAY BY THE *RULES*. WE HAVE AN *ETHICAL CODE* WE HAVE TO FOLLOW. EVERYTHING *WE* DO IS PUT UNDER A *MICROSCOPE*.
BUT *THEM?* THE THINGS *THEY* DID TO US IN THAT CAMP, THE THINGS OTHERS *LIKE* THEM DO TO OUR G.I.'S?
IT'S BARBARIC.
SKRAK
AND STILL THE CYNICIS FALLS ON *US*
NO ONE KNOWS WHA WE'VE GONE THROUGH.
NO ONE BUT EACH OTHER.
RING. SCAN VITALS.
SCANNING.
WH... WHERE?
YOU'RE GOING TO BE SAFE, MISS. I'M GOING TO TAKE YOU HOME.
WAIT.

HAL?
I'M SO SORRY.
YOU DON'T HAVE TO BE.
VITALS STABLE.

FUMP
RRR
VUTT
VUTT
VUTT
WARNING. FORCE FIELD BREACHED. TRANQUILIZER DETECTED.
MY SIDE STARTS TO GO NUMB.
MORE BOUNTY HUNTERS.
DOMINATORS TOO. SHREWD, ARROGANT, AND THEY SMELL LIKE FRESH TAR.
HIS BRAIN IS SMALL. HIS CENTRAL NERVOUS SYSTEM SIMPLE.
THEY'RE TRYING TO TAKE ME DOWN LIKE AN ANIMAL, BUT THE RING'S ALREADY COUNTERACTING THE SEDATIVES.
I DON'T HAVE TIM TO BE NUMB.
CONTACT LORAGG. TELL HIM WE HAVE THE LANTERN.

SKRAK
I NEED TO GET HER HOME.
ROARG NARK HAKK!
THESE BOUNTY HUNTERS ARE COMIN' OUTTA THE WOODWORK.
WHAT THE--
BOOM
BACK OFF, DOMINATORS! HE'S MINE!
KZZZZTT
AARH!
RING'S GOING CRAZY--
I'VE BEEN TRACKING YOU FOR WEEKS. I'VE RECORDED YOUR BRAIN'S WAVELENGTH--AND NOW I'M SENDING OUT A DOZEN DIFFERENT THOUGHTS ACROSS IT.
YOUR RING'S AS CONFUSED AS YOU ARE.

YOU BELONG TO HUNGER DOG NOW, GUARDIAN SCUM.
SKRAK
LORAGG. I PICKED UP WHAT THE FACELESS HUNTERS COULDN'T KEEP. I'VE GOT THE GREEN LANTERN.
AS SOON AS I HAVE D.N.A. VERIFICATION I'LL SEND YOU THE DROP-OFF POINT.
GET THE HELL AWAY FROM HIM.
HE'S WITH A HUMAN.
MY EMPLOYER SAYS THERE'S AN EXTRA ROTOX IN IT IF YOU SPILL OUT HER INSIDES.
SHINGGG
LET'S MAKE IT TWO, LORAGG.

COWGIRL...?
SHE'S DEAD.
SHE CRASHED IN A FOREIGN LAND AND DIED WITHOUT HER FAMILY. IT'S ALMOST *IRONIC,* REALLY.
MY *FATHER* CRASHED HIS SHIP ON THIS VERY SPOT. HE DIED WITHOUT HIS FAMILY TOO.
YOUR MILITARY STOLE HIS SHIP. *YOU* STOLE HIS RING.
THEN *YOU* BURIED HIS BODY SOMEWHERE IN THIS VAST DESERT.
YOU'RE GOING TO TAKE ME TO THAT SPOT, *HAL JORDAN.* YOU'RE GOING TO DIG UP *ABIN SUR'S* UNMARKED GRAVE.

AND THEN I'M GOING TO BURY YOU IN IT.

Green Lantern #17
Cover art by **Ivan Reis**
and **Oclair Albert**

WANTED: HAL JORDAN

Chapter Four

GOTHAM CITY.
KRAKK
HAS ANYONE HEARD FROM JORDAN?
NOT SINCE YESTERDAY...
...BUT HE WAS RIGHT ABOUT THE GLOBAL GUARDIANS. J'ONN'S FILTERED THEIR BRAINS FREE OF THE FACELESS HUNTERS' PROGRAMMING.
AND ALAN SCOTT'S WITH CHECKMATE, MAKING SURE ALL MURDER CHARGES AGAINST HAL HAVE BEEN DROPPED...THOUGH RUSSIA IS INSISTING THAT WE OWE THE ROCKET RED BRIGADE A FORMAL APOLOGY.
ROCKET RED ONE HELD HIS OWN AND KEPT HIS COOL.
AND WE'VE BEEN THINKING ABOUT EXPANDING THE LEAGUE.
I'LL PASS ALONG THE IDEA TO WONDER WOMAN.
YOU HEAR ANYTHING FROM JORDAN, YOU LET ME KNOW.
HE MIGHT STILL NEED OUR HELP.
BATMAN OUT.
HAVE A GOOD NIGHT.
Nn.
BRUCE WAYNE OF THE PLANET EARTH.
YOU HAVE THE ABILITY TO INSTILL GREAT FEAR.

WELCOME TO THE SINESTRO CORPS.

THE WHAT?
YOU HAVE BEEN CHOSEN TO REPRESENT SPACE SECTOR 2814.
FZZP
-AARRRGHHH-!
BRUCE WAYNE.
YOU WILL NOW BE SUBJECTED TO--
N-NO...
CONFLICTING EMOTIONAL RESONANCE REGISTERED. WILLPOWER OVERRIDING FEAR.
PREVIOUS EXPOSURE TO GREEN LANTERN POWER RING DETECTED.
GET OFF!
TARGET SENTIENT REJECTED.
SHRAKK
SECTOR SCAN FOR REPLACEMENT SENTIENT INITIATED.
WHAT THE HELL WAS *THAT?*

THE SIERRA MADRES.
WHERE DID YOU BURY MY FATHER?

YOU'RE ABIN SUR'S SON?
MY RING'S NOT RESPONDING.
YOU CAN'T HURT ME, HAL JORDAN. YOU HAVE NO POWER.
WHEN I RETRIEVED MY FATHER'S SHIP FROM EDWARDS AIR FORCE BASE, I TOOK WHAT WAS LEFT OF THEIR IMPRISONED MANHUNTER--
--AND I USED ITS POWER BATTERY SKULL TO DEPLETE THE RING.
I DELIVERED HIM TO YOU. I KILLED THAT HUMAN GIRL. I NEED TO GET PAID.
AS SOON AS THIS IS OVER, HUNGER DOG.
EVEN WITH THE RING EMPTY, AMON, WE STILL CAN'T REMOVE IT.
IT WILL REMOVE ITSELF ONCE HAL JORDAN IS DEAD, LORAGG. UNTIL THEN, HE REMAINS POWERLESS.
POWERLESS? I DON'T NEED THE RING TO KICK YOUR--
KRAK
NGGG
YOU DON'T NEED THE RING?
MY FATHER PASSED ALONG HIS MOST PRECIOUS HEIRLOOM TO YOU, AND YOU TREAT IT WITH SUCH...LEVITY?!
THE RING CAN'T POSSIBLY MEAN THAT MUCH TO YOU.
BUT TO ME, IT MEANS EVERYTHING.

"MY FATHER LEFT OUR HOMEWORLD OF UNGARA BEFORE HE KNEW MY MOTHER WAS PREGNANT.
"HE NEVER RETURNED TO US.
"IT TOOK YEARS FOR THE GREEN LANTERN CORPS TO FINALLY SEND SOMEONE TO NOTIFY MY MOTHER AND ME OF HIS DEATH.
"AND IT WASN'T EVEN ABIN SUR'S REPLACEMENT.
"I DOUBT SOMEONE AS SELF-IMPORTANT AS YOU EVEN CONSIDERED THAT ABIN SUR HAD A FAMILY OUTSIDE OF THE CORPS.
IN MEMORIAM
"I SPENT MY LIFE LIVING IN MY FATHER'S SHADOW. AT FIRST, I RESENTED HIM FOR IT.
"SO I THOUGHT I'D FOUND A WAY TO MAKE MY OWN NAME WHEN I JOINED THE BLACK CIRCLE CRIME SYNDICATE.
"BUT KYLE RAYNER INTERFERED IN OUR ACTIVITIES WHEN EARTH BECAME INVOLVED.
"DURING OUR NEXT CONFRONTATION--
"--MY HEAD WAS BLOWN OFF."

YOUR HEAD?
NOT ALL RACES ARE AS VULNERABLE TO CRANIAL INJURY AS TERRESTRIALS.
SO YOU WENT AFTER KYLE FOR HIS RING AND NOW YOU'RE AFTER MINE.
I OBTAINED KYLE RAYNER'S RING BRIEFLY. BUT...
...IT DID NOT WORK FOR ME.
AND YOU THINK THIS ONE WILL?
YES.
BECAUSE I'M NOT AFRAID ANYMORE.
RIGHT HERE.
I BURIED HIM RIGHT HERE.

TZZZAK
SHOOM

THINGS SHOULD HAVE BEEN DIFFERENT.
I SHOULD HAVE BEEN DIFFERENT.
MY FATHER WAS NEVER THERE FOR ME. HE WAS NEVER THERE BECAUSE OF THE DAMN GREEN LANTERN CORPS.
WHAT I BECAME FOR SO LONG WAS THEIR FAULT.

YOU'VE GOT TO BE KIDDING ME.
YOU DON'T GET A FREE PASS BECAUSE YOUR FATHER WASN'T THERE.
NO ONE ELSE DID.
DO IT, AMON! KILL HIM!
LISTEN TO THE BUG. THIS IS WHAT YOU'VE BEEN PLANNING ANYWAY, RIGHT?
THIS IS THE BIG TEST.
YOU WANT TO PROVE YOU'RE AS FEARLESS AS YOUR FATHER.
I AM FEARLESS.
YOU'RE A COWARD.
YOU DIDN'T STEP OUT OF THE SHADOWS UNTIL YOUR BOUNTY HUNTERS BEAT ME DOWN. YOU STILL HAVE HUNGER DOG HERE IN CASE I FIGHT BACK.
AND YOUR HAND'S SHAKING.

I EXECUTED *THOUSANDS* WHEN I WAS EXPELLED FROM THE BLACK CIRCLE.

I HUNTED DOWN EVERY MEMBER-- I TRACKED DOWN THEIR FAMILIES.

KRAK

I SLAUGHTERED EVERY SINGLE ONE OF THEM.

I WAS NOT AFRAID OF THEM!

THEY WERE AFRAID OF *ME!*
TZZZAK

FZZZAK
YOU WERE SUPPOSED TO GIVE ME A *SIGN* BEFORE STARTING TROUBLE, JORDAN.

AND THAT SIGN WASN'T GETTING YOUR ASS FRIED.

SOMEONE CALL FOR BACKUP?
HIS NAME IS JOHN STEWART.
HE'S MY PARTNER.

ANOTHER LANTERN, AMON!
RUN! RUN--
THOOOOM
TWO MONTHS AGO, JOHN WENT UNDERCOVER TO FIND OUT WHO PUT A PRICE ON MY HEAD.
HE CAPTURED THE REAL HUNGER DOG, THREW HIM TO GARDNER ON OA, AND TOOK THE BOUNTY HUNTER'S PLACE.
THREE HOURS AGO, JOHN MET UP WITH ME IN RUSSIA. HE COULD ONLY CONTACT WHOEVER WAS BEHIND THE BOUNTY HUNTERS IF HE HAD ME WRAPPED UP WITH A BOW.
WE SPOKE THROUGH OUR RINGS AND I AGREED TO LET HIM KNOCK ME UNCONSCIOUS.
I PUT MY LIFE-- AND COWGIRL'S-- IN HIS HANDS. THAT WASN'T HARD.
TAKING A BACK SEAT TO THE ACTION, ON THE OTHER HAND...
YOU ALWAYS KNOW HOW TO PUSH THEIR BUTTONS.
BOOM
THAT'S THE FUN PART.
I'LL WRAP THIS UP.
COOL YOUR RING, JOHN.
BOOM
BOOM

THIS IS *YOUR FAULT,* HAL JORDAN.
YOU TOOK EVERYTHING MY FATHER WAS--
WHAM
THIS PUNK IS MINE!
--AND LEFT ME WITH *NOTHING.*
KRAK

KEEP FIGHTING.
I GOT IT--

WHAT IS IT?

AMON SUR OF THE PLANET UNGARA.

YOU HAVE THE ABILITY TO INSTILL GREAT FEAR.

KRAKOOOOM

AIIEEE!

WELCOME TO THE SINESTRO CORPS.

SINESTRO CORPS?
DID YOU HEAR THAT VOICE?
YOU HAVE BEEN CHOSEN TO REPRESENT SPACE SECTOR 2814.
I'VE BEEN...
CHOSEN.
I CAN FEEL IT BUBBLING OUT OF ME...
...SCRATCHING ACROSS MY SKIN...

AARRRGH!!
YES.
DO YOU SEE ME NOW, FATHER?
DO YOU SEE WHAT I CAN DO?
SKOOOM
NO MORE HIDING IN YOUR SHADOW.
I'VE MOVED INTO THE LIGHT!
AMON SUR.

YOU WILL NOW BE SUBJECTED TO PSYCHOLOGICAL AND PHYSICAL RECONDITIONING.
WHAT?
STOP!
A POWER RING OBEYS ITS OWNER!
PREPARING TO TRANSPORT SENTIENT BEING.
YOU OBEY ME, RING! YOU OBEY M--
--EEEEARRRGHHHH!
I BETTER NOTIFY SALAKK.
YEAH.
OKAY.

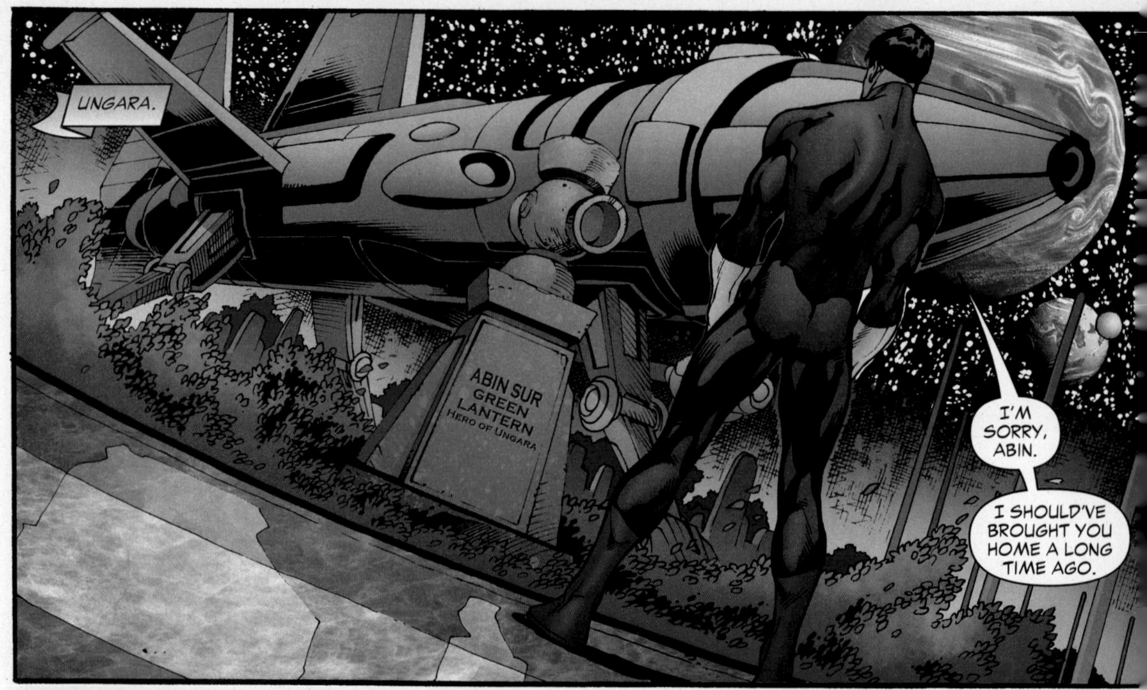
UNGARA.
ABIN SUR
GREEN
LANTERN
HERO OF UNGARA
I'M SORRY, ABIN.
I SHOULD'VE BROUGHT YOU HOME A LONG TIME AGO.

ABIN SUR
GREEN

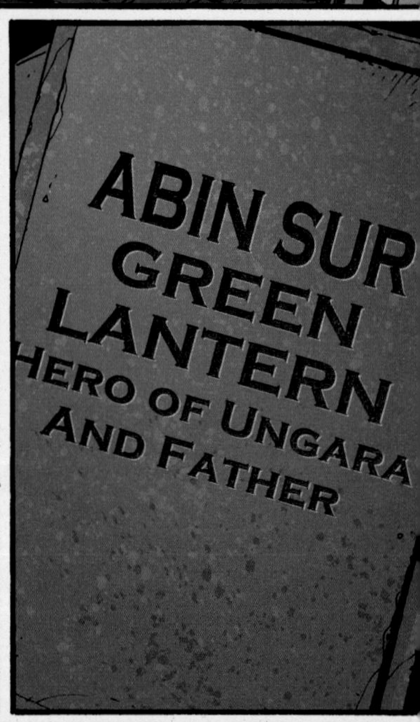
ABIN SUR
GREEN
LANTERN
HERO OF UNGARA
AND FATHER

ABIN SUR
GREEN
LANTERN
HERO OF UNGARA
AND FATHER

ABIN SUR
GREEN
LANTERN
HERO OF UNGARA
AND FATHER

EDWARDS AIR FORCE BASE.
I SHOULD'VE BEEN HERE.
A LOT OF GOOD MEN AND WOMEN GOT HURT.
YA CAN'T BE EVERYWHERE AT ONCE, SUPER-HERO.
I'M GLAD YOU'RE OKAY, COWGIRL.
TAKE CARE OF YOURSELF.
HEY.
DON'T YA THINK WE GOT SOMETHIN' ELSE TO JAW ABOUT...
...HAL?
LOVE DAD

NORTHERN CALIFORNIA.
FERRIS AIR
Exit 5 Miles
BWHAKOOOM
WHICH BODY DOES MY CHOSEN MATE DESIRE?
I THINK I KNOW.

Green Lantern #18
Cover art by **Ivan Reis** and **Oclair Albert**

MYSTERY OF THE STAR SAPPHIRE
Chapter One

SOUTHERN CALIFORNIA.

FERRIS AIR.

WHAT WOULD YOU GIVE UP FOR LOVE?

TOM KALMAKU HAD A SHOT AT BECOMING MUCH MORE THAN AN ENGINEER. THE GUARDIANS OF THE UNIVERSE OFFERED HIM POWER LIKE HIS IDOL AND FRIEND HAL JORDAN.

TOM SAID, AND I QUOTE, "NAW."

HE USED TO REMINISCE ABOUT HIS ADVENTURES AS GREEN LANTERN'S "SIDEKICK." NOW ALL HE TALKS ABOUT ARE HIS ADVENTURES AS A FATHER.

SHE'LL BE HERE ANY SECOND.

YOUR BOSS ***USED*** TO BE A SHARK OF A BUSINESSWOMAN. NOW SHE'S AT LEAST THIRTY MINUTES ***LATE*** FOR EVERY MEETING.

SHE'S GOT HER HEAD IN THE CLOUDS!

HER FATHER MUST BE ROLLING IN HIS GRAVE.

WHERE ***IS*** SHE, TOM?

WHERE SHE BELONGS.
THIS IS TOWER TO LADY FERRIS. YOU GOT A BUNCHA SUITS WAITIN' FOR YA DOWN HERE.
TOM'S DRESSED UP TOO, THOUGH I WOULDN'T SAY HE LOOKS NATURAL WITHOUT GREASE ON HIS SHIRT.
TOM'S ABOUT TO BECOME AN EQUAL PARTNER, TOWER. HE CAN WEAR THAT SUIT FOR ONE DAY.
ROGER THAT.

MY NAME IS CAROL FERRIS.
YOU ARE CLEARED FOR LANDING.
THANK YOU, TOWER.
I USED TO BE GREEN LANTERN'S GIRLFRIEND.

THE FIRST TIME I MET HAL JORDAN, I WAS SEVEN YEARS OLD.
HIS FATHER WAS A TEST PILOT WHO WORKED FOR MINE.
MARTIN JORDAN CRASHED RIGHT IN FRONT OF US.
I NEVER WANTED TO BE A SUIT, BUT WHEN MY FATHER GOT SICK IT WAS THAT OR LOSE FERRIS AIR ALTOGETHER.
IT WASN'T A DISEASE THAT GOT MY FATHER SICK. IT WAS THE GUILT.
HE BLAMED HIMSELF FOR MARTIN JORDAN'S CRASH.
THAT'S WHY WHEN HAL WAS DISHONORABLY DISCHARGED FROM THE AIR FORCE MY FATHER INSISTED I HIRE HIM.
HE WAS THE MOST ARROGANT MAN I'D EVER MET. I TRIED TO KEEP HAL ON THE GROUND, BUT MY FATHER INSISTED I LET HIM FLY, TOO.
THAT'S WHY THERE WAS SO MUCH TENSION BETWEEN US.
I WANTED TO BE IN THE AIR.
EVENTUALLY, HE TOOK ME WITH HIM.
THE MAN AND THE WOMAN WHO DIDN'T HAVE TIME TO FALL IN LOVE DID.
THEN PARALLAX HAPPENED.
I THOUGHT HAL DIED.
AND I MARRIED SOMEONE ELSE.

I HAD TO LET HAL GO.
AT LEAST, THAT'S WHAT I TELL MYSELF.
WHAT THE--?
KRRRKKSHH
CAROL FERRIS.
BODY OF DESIRE.
KKK.
I MISSED YOU, PRINCESS.

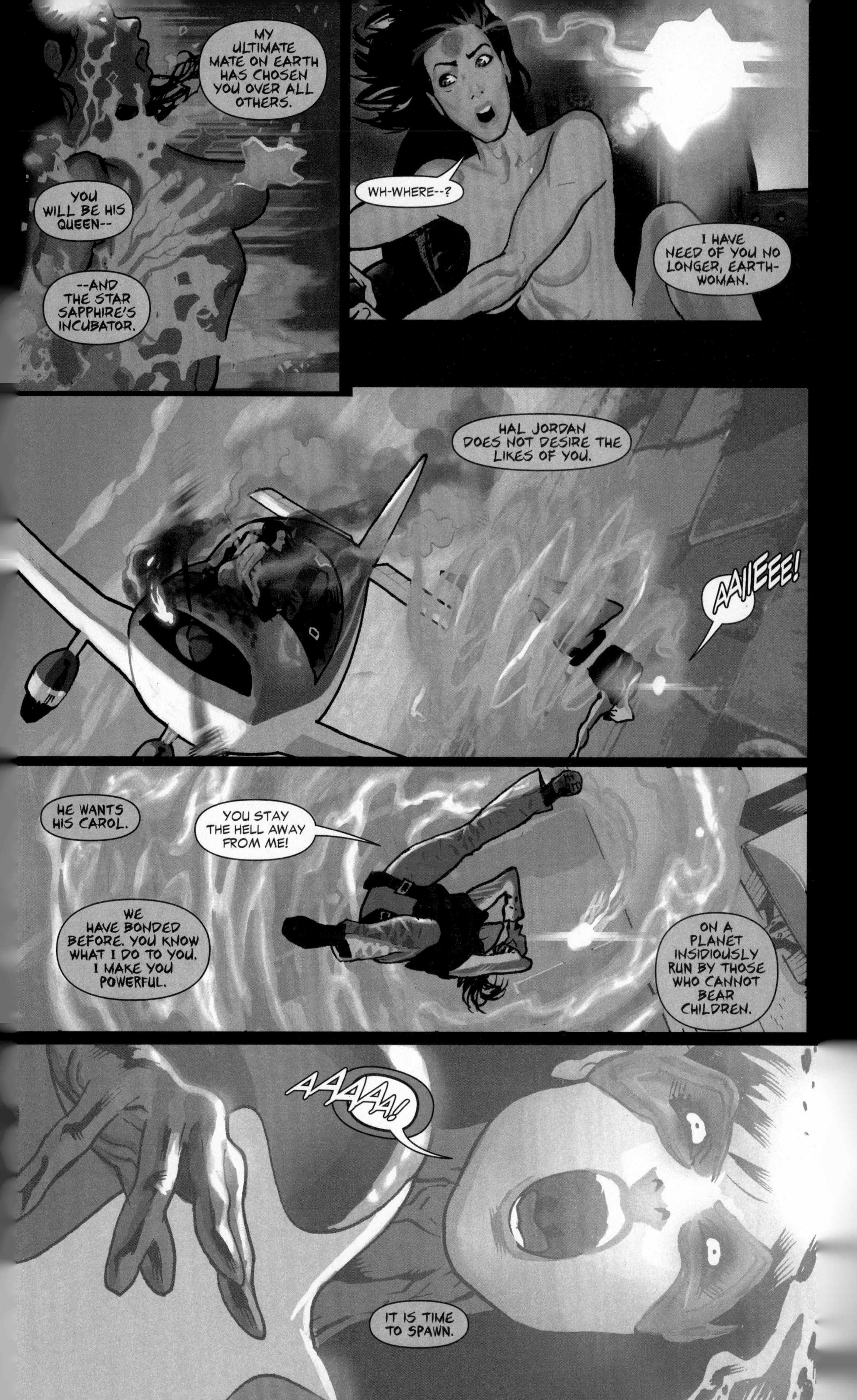
MY ULTIMATE MATE ON EARTH HAS CHOSEN YOU OVER ALL OTHERS.
YOU WILL BE HIS QUEEN--
--AND THE STAR SAPPHIRE'S INCUBATOR.
WH-WHERE--?
I HAVE NEED OF YOU NO LONGER, EARTH-WOMAN.
HAL JORDAN DOES NOT DESIRE THE LIKES OF YOU.
AAIIEEE!
HE WANTS HIS CAROL.
YOU STAY THE HELL AWAY FROM ME!
WE HAVE BONDED BEFORE. YOU KNOW WHAT I DO TO YOU. I MAKE YOU POWERFUL.
ON A PLANET INSIDIOUSLY RUN BY THOSE WHO CANNOT BEAR CHILDREN.
AAAAA!
IT IS TIME TO SPAWN.

IT IS TIME FOR LOVE.

EDWARDS AIR FORCE BASE.
PANCHO'S.
IT'S TRUE LOVE, AIN'T IT?
WHAT IS, COWGIRL?
YOU AND THAT RING OF YOURS.
WHEN YA PUT IT ON, EVERYTHING THAT KEEPS YA DOWN EVAPORATES. EVERY WORRY YA GOT DRIES UP.
THAT'S HOW I FEEL WHEN I FLY, HIGH BALL.
'COURSE IT TAKES ME FIFTEEN MILLION DOLLARS' WORTH OF EQUIPMENT TA DO IT.

SO WHO ELSE KNOWS THE DIRTY LITTLE SECRET?
GENERAL STONE.
THE BOSS? FIGURES. NO OTHER WAY YOU COULD BE ABSENT SO MUCH AND STAY IN THE FORCE.
WHAT ABOUT ROCKET-MAN?
NO. NOT YET ANYWAY.
I OWE HIM SOMETHING. AT LEAST SOME KIND OF AN APOLOGY.
HE LOST HIS CHANCE TO GET INTO NASA BECAUSE OF WHAT THOSE TERRORISTS DID TO HIS LEG.
HE'S STILL ALIVE. AND HE'S GOT A GOOD FAMILY.
IF I'D BEEN WEARING MY RING WE WOULDN'T HAVE BEEN IN THAT CAMP FOR MORE THAN TWO MINUTES.
ALL THOSE MONTHS WE WERE LOCKED UP...ARE *MY* FAULT.
YOU DIDN'T SHOOT OUR PLANES DOWN, HIGH BALL.
YOU DIDN'T LOCK US IN THOSE CELLS.
YA JUST LIKE THE RUSH OF LIVIN' WITH NO SAFETY NET. THAT *AIN'T* A CRIME.
TA TELL YA THE TRUTH, IF I HAD ONE OF THEM *TRINKETS* I WOULDN'T WEAR IT WHEN I FLEW EITHER.
'COURSE, I'VE *NEVER* WORN A RING.

STILL. YOU AND I ARE A LOT ALIKE, COWBOY.
TOO ALIKE, DON'T YOU THINK?
AH, COME ON NOW. THE GREEN LANTERN'S NOT SUPPOSED TO BE SCARED OF ANYTHIN'.
DON'T TELL ME YOU'RE SCARED OF ME, SUPER-HERO.
MAYBE JUST A LITTLE.

BABOOOMM
YOU'RE NOT CHEATING ON ME, ARE YOU?
YES.
KRAKKAKKL
BACK OFF, JEM.
SMASH

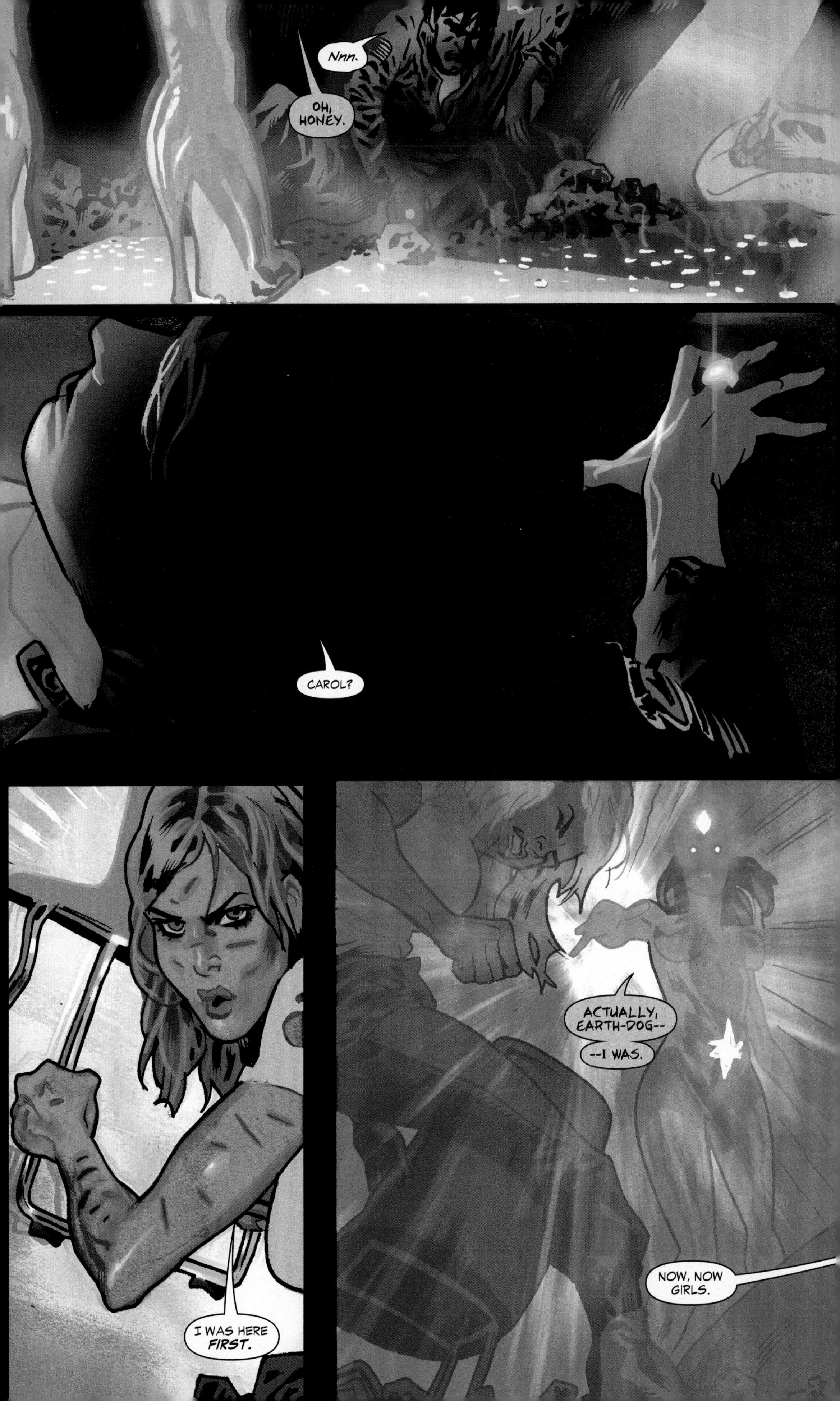

Nnn.
OH, HONEY.
CAROL?
I WAS HERE FIRST.
ACTUALLY, EARTH-DOG--
--I WAS.
NOW, NOW GIRLS.

THERE'S ENOUGH OF ME TO GO AROUND.
A QUEEN DOES NOT SHARE.

WHOOOM!
WHO IS THAT?
AN EX-GIRLFRIEND.
SHE ALWAYS THIS BITCHY?
ONLY WHEN SHE'S POSSESSED BY A TELEPATHIC ALIEN CRYSTAL.
WELL, AND WHEN SHE DOESN'T HAVE COFFEE.
WHAT DOES SHE WANT?
UM...ONE LAST FLING, I THINK. BUT I CAN'T DO THAT--
--SHE'S MARRIED.
SHE SURE DON'T ACT LIKE IT.

I FEEL A CONFLICT.
KRRAZZT
CAROL.
HANG TIGHT. I'M GOING TO PRY THAT ROCK OFF OF YOU.
YOUR HEART BEATS FOR ANOTHER.
HER.
KKRRKKLL
AAAAA!
OH, NO.
YOU'RE NOT GONNA--
JILLIAN PEARLMAN.
YOU ARE ALSO A BODY HE DESIRES.

I'VE GOT YOU, CAROL.
HAL?
WHY DO YOU RUN? I HAVE READ YOUR MIND. YOU WILL ENJOY THIS.
YOU WANT HIM AS MUCH AS I DO.
I SAW IT ALL THIS TIME, HAL. I KNOW WHAT THE STAR SAPPHIRE IS.
SECTOR 1416. THEY COME FROM SECTOR 1416.
THEY?
THE ZAMARONS... SINESTRO...
MMMM.
TELL ME, HAL...

...DO YA WANT THIS BODY INSTEAD?
IT'S AWFULLY YUMMY.
BAR

Green Lantern #19
Cover art by **Ivan Reis** and **Oclair Albert**

MYSTERY OF THE STAR SAPPHIRE
Chapter Two

I KNOW YOU WANT ME. I WANT IT TOO, HAL JORDAN.
I WANT THIS WHOLE PLANET. BUT FIRST--
--I WANT YOU TO DROP THE BRUNETTE!
YOU GOT MARRIED.
YOU WERE DEAD.
NOT THAT LONG.
FSSNAP
SO HOW LONG HAVE YOU TWO BEEN DATING?
ME AND COWGIRL?
COWGIRL? LET ME TAKE A GUESS WHERE YOU MET--
IT'S HER CALL SIGN. AND WE WERE ONLY HAVING A DRINK.
WHICH IS A DATE.

FZZAP
OUR UNION WILL BE PLEASURABLE.
YOU'VE CHOSEN THE BODY OF CAPTAIN JILLIAN PEARLMAN, HAVEN'T YOU? SO I'VE TAKEN IT. I'M YOURS.
WHY DO YOU STILL PLAY GAMES, HAL JORDAN?
I'VE GOT TO GET THAT ROCK OFF HER.
I MIGHT NOT HAVE BEEN IN CONTROL WHEN I WAS STAR SAPPHIRE, BUT I REMEMBER EVERY MOVE SHE MADE, HAL.
AND I REMEMBER HER MEMORIES. THERE'S MORE THAN ONE OF THOSE THINGS.
I CAN JUGGLE MORE THAN ONE.
THE STAR SAPPHIRES ARE LIKE THE RINGS, HAL. THE GREEN RINGS--
--AND THE YELLOW ONES.
YELLOW? HOW DID YOU--
I DON'T KNOW, BUT THERE'S A WAR COMING. AND THE STAR SAPPHIRES ARE CONNECTED TO IT...

"...YOU ONCE TOLD ME IT STARTED BILLIONS OF YEARS AGO.
"AFTER WITNESSING THE 'ORIGIN' OF THE UNIVERSE, THE GUARDIANS DECIDED TO FORM A CORPS TO POLICE IT.
"BUT I SAW OTHER THINGS HAPPENING THERE."
<THE BOOK OF OA WILL PROTECT US.>
<WE CAN NEVER BECOME VICTIMS OF THE EMOTIONAL SPECTRUM THAT HAS BEEN BORN OUT OF LIFE'S SENTIENCE.>
<PROTECT US, GANTHET?! THE LAWS WITHIN THE BOOK YOU ALL HAVE WRITTEN DEMAND WE CLEANSE OURSELVES OF EMOTION!>
<YOU HAVE SEEN THE DESTRUCTION PARALLAX HAS CAUSED-->
<YES, AND LIFE WITHOUT FEAR IS ADMIRABLE.>
<BUT LIFE WITHOUT LOVE OR COMPASSION OR HOPE IS BLASPHEMY.>
"WHILE MOST DECLARED THEMSELVES THE GUARDIANS OF THE UNIVERSE AND CREATED THE GREEN LANTERN CORPS--
"--A TRIBE OF WOMEN LEFT OA."
<WHAT YOU ABANDON, WE SHALL GATHER.>
<BEGINNING WITH LOVE.>

TRIBE VENTURED ACROSS THE UNIVERSE, SEARCHING FOR WHAT THE GUARDIANS FEARED.
"IN SECTOR 1416, ON A PLANET CALLED ZAMARON, THEY THOUGHT THEY FOUND SOMETHING...
"...GROWING ACROSS THE EMBRACED SKELETONS OF AN ADAM AND EVE ON A WORLD LONG DEAD."
<SISTERS.>
<THEIR DYING LOVE HAS GIVEN BIRTH TO THE VIOLET LIGHT.>
<WE SHALL SHED LOVE'S LIGHT ACROSS THE UNIVERSE-->
SKAZZAK
AAAIEEE!!
"IT TOOK DAYS TO FREE HER.
"THE ZAMARON TRIBE STARTED THE EXPERIMENTS NOT LONG AFTER."

"THE MORNING I BECAME ONE OF THEM, MY FATHER AND I HAD A FIGHT. I WAS TIRED OF RUNNING NUMBERS AND BEING CHAINED TO MY DESK.
"SO I ESCAPED INTO THE AIR.
LADY CAROL
"I HEARD VOICES UP THERE. THE PLANE FELL. I BLACKED OUT.
"WHEN I WOKE UP, THE ZAMARONS WERE STANDING OVER ME.
"THEY MADE ME SEE THEM...
"...AS I SAW MYSELF."
YOU HAVE BEEN CHOSEN, CAROL FERRIS OF EARTH.
"I KNEW WHAT THE PILOTS AND ENGINEERS THOUGHT."
YOU WILL BE THE QUEEN.
"DADDY'S SPOILED LITTLE GIRL."
QUEEN OF EARTH.
"QUEEN FERRIS."

"THE STAR SAPPHIRE TOOK OVER.
"WE NEVER REALLY KNEW WHAT IT WAS, BUT WE KNEW WHAT IT DID TO ME.
"IT TOOK CONTROL."
BUT MY RING CAN OVERRIDE IT. WE TIRE HER OUT, I'LL BE ABLE TO REMOVE IT.
BUT THE SAPPHIRE ALWAYS COMES BACK--
"--UNTIL IT FINDS SOMEONE ELSE."
...DON'T HAVE TO SAY YOU'RE GOING TO CALL IF YOU'RE NOT, HAL.
IT WAS FUN WHILE IT LASTED.
IT WAS, DEB. TAKE CARE.
"AFTER ME, THERE WAS DEBORAH CAMILLE DARNELL, A STEWARDESS AT FERRIS AIR."
HAL JORDAN DOESN'T LOVE YOU, DEBORAH.
WHAT--
BUT HE WILL.
"THE STAR SAPPHIRE WENT AFTER WHOEVER YOU WERE INTIMATE WITH.
"AND THOUGH YOU MIGHT'VE FOUGHT IT O TIME AFTER TIME--"

"--NOT EVERYONE DID.
"ON THE PLANET XANADOR, THERE WAS ANOTHER GREEN LANTERN. AND HIS ALIEN LOVER, DELA PHARON.
"THE ZAMARONS DELIVERED A STAR SAPPHIRE TO HER.
"THE TWO MATED.
"SHE KILLED HIM THAT NIGHT.
"THEN THE SPAWN BEGAN."
SPACE SECTOR SCAN 1416 FOR REPLACEMENT SENTIENT INITIATED.
"THE SAPPHIRE INVADED EVERY LIVING CELL ON THE PLANET.
"CRYSTALS GREW ACROSS THE WORLD."

"UNTIL XANADOR WAS PROTECTED."
⟨THE EXPERIMENT IS A SUCCESS.⟩
⟨LOVE IS UNDER OUR CONTROL.⟩
⟨LOVE WILL PRESERVE ALL OF LIFE.⟩
...CHASELON OF BARRIO III, YOU HAVE BEEN CHOSEN...
⟨THE POWER RING OF SECTOR 1416 HAS CHOSEN ANOTHER.⟩
⟨LET THE GUARDIANS FIGHT THEIR ENDLESS BATTLES--⟩
⟨--WE WILL PREVENT THE WARS OF THE FUTURE.⟩
⟨WE WILL SPREAD LOVE THROUGHOUT THE UNIVERSE.⟩
"IS THAT WHAT THE ZAMARONS THINK LOVE IS, CAROL?
"ENCASING LIFE IN CRYSTAL? PUTTING IT IN SUSPENDED ANIMATION?"

LOVE ISN'T ABOUT CONTROL.
THE ZAMARONS THINK IT IS, HAL.
THEY'VE BEEN ISOLATED IN THE CRYSTAL CAVERNS OF ZAMARON FOR BILLIONS OF YEARS.
THEY'VE TWISTED WHAT LOVE MEANS.
AND WHAT DOES IT MEAN?
YOU NEVER EVEN LIKED TO SAY THE WORD.
ACTIONS SPEAK LOUDER THAN WORDS, CAROL.
FOR YOU, MAYBE.
SO--THIS COWGIRL?
SHE SOMEONE SPECIAL?
...
YES.

ENOUGH TEASING!
LET'S FIND A SPOT.
SKOOM
HoneyMoo
HOTEL
THOOM
WHAT DO YOU LOVE, HAL JORDAN?
Nnn...

DO YOU LOVE EARTH?
FUMP
DO YOU LOVE THIS RING?

DO YOU LOVE ME?
I DON'T DO THIS ON THE FIRST DATE, COWGIRL.
OH, SUGAR...

YOU'VE NEVER MET GREEN ARROW.
FWAM
SKASH
GET OUT OF HERE.
MAKE ME A SUIT.
WHAT?
I DIDN'T CONTROL MYSELF WHEN I WAS THE STAR SAPPHIRE, BUT I SAW HER FIGHT.
I LEARNED HOW TO FIGHT.
LIGHT ME UP.
I KEPT CAROL FERRIS ALIVE IN CASE YOU CHANGED YOUR MIND AGAIN--
--BUT NOW I SHALL BURN HER PALE FLESH--

DON'T WRITE CHECKS YOUR ASS CAN'T CASH, HONEY.
BOOOMM
WHOOM
GREEN REALLY ISN'T YOUR COLOR.

AND PINK ISN'T YOURS.
IF YOU CAN HEAR ME--
--SORRY ABOUT THIS, COWGIRL.
WHAM
AAH!
HAL...HAL, WHAT'S GOING ON?
WHY ARE YOU DOING THIS?
COME ON NOW, STAR.
DON'T ROLEPLAY.
I KNOW YOU'RE IN CONTROL UNTIL THE JEWEL COMES OFF.
I'LL BE ANYONE YOU WANT.
YOU GOT HER?
YEAH.
CAN I HIT HER ONE MORE TIME?
NO.
...SHE GOING TO BE OKAY?

I HOPE SO.
HAL, I NEED TO TELL YOU...
THE NEW CORPS IS RISING.
WHAT IS--?
WARNING. HIGH ENERGY SIGNATURE DETECTED.
SO MUST OURS.

STARTING WITH THESE TWO.
NOW LOWER YOUR RING, GUARDIAN DOG, AND LET LOVE PROTECT YOU.
AND HERE I THOUGHT OUR FIRST DATE WAS GONNA BE WEIRD.
NICE HELMETS, BY THE WAY.

Green Lantern #20
Cover art by **Ivan Reis**
and **Oclair Albert**

MYSTERY OF THE STAR SAPPHIRE
Chapter Three

"THAT'S HAL JORDAN.
"MY EX-BOYFRIEND.
"I'M CAROL FERRIS.
"HIS EX-GIRLFRIEND.
"WE'RE IN THE PARKING GARAGE OF THE 'HONEYMOON HOTEL.' WOULD YOU BELIEVE THIS IS THE CLOSEST WE EVER GOT TO THAT KIND OF THING?"
SIT TIGHT, CAROL.
I'LL GET US OUT OF HERE.
"AND HE CAN'T WAIT TO LEAVE."
WITH COWGIRL UNCONSCIOUS, AND THE FIGHT SHE PUT UP, THE STAR SAPPHIRE'S WEAKENED. SEE IF YOU CAN PRY THE ROCK OFF HER--
WHAT ABOUT COWGIRL?

--THE ONES THAT UNLEASHED IT AREN'T GONNA GIVE ME THE CHANCE.
FWAM
"THESE ALIEN AMAZONS ARE AN OFFSHOOT TRIBE OF THE GUARDIANS.
"WHILE THE GUARDIANS TURNED THEIR BACK ON EMOTIONS, THE ZAMARONS SET OUT TO EMBRACE THEM.
"THEY THOUGHT THEY DID WHEN THEY STARTED CULTIVATING THE POWER THE PARASITIC STAR SAPPHIRES TAP INTO. THEY CALL IT THE 'VIOLET LIGHT OF LOVE.'
"THE ZAMARONS HAVE SHOWN UP OVER THE YEARS, MOSTLY TOSSING THE PARASITES *MY* WAY.
"BUT THIS TIME THE STAR SAPPHIRE FOUND A *NEW* HOST. ONE IT THOUGHT HAL WAS MORE INTERESTED IN..."
BETTER BITE DOWN ON SOMETHING, BLONDIE--
KKKKK
--THIS IS GOING TO STING.

SKRAK
THESE WOMEN HAVE A HIGHER PURPOSE, GREEN LANTERN.
THEY WILL BE THE FIRST OF OUR ANGELS.
KOOM
DO YOU LOVE THEM?
DO YOU LOVE THEM BOTH?
KRAKL
IF YOU DO, GIVE THEM TO US. IF THEY ACCEPT THE STAR SAPPHIRE INTO THEIR LIVES, THEY WILL NEVER GROW OLD.
THEY WILL BE IMMORTAL, AS WE ARE. AS WILL THE WORLDS THEY WATCH OVER.
YOU MEAN THE WORLDS YOU WANT THEM TO ENCASE IN CRYSTAL. INCLUDING EARTH.
HAVEN'T YOU HEARD THE SAYING, "IF YOU TRULY LOVE SOMETHING--
"--SET IT FREE"?
KRAKK
AAAAAHH!

HOTEL
I READ IT ON A GREETING CARD.
JUST
Hnnn.
HERE.
PUT SOME CLOTHES ON.
MY HEAD'S KILLIN' ME.
THE SAPPHIRE'S WORSE THAN THE MORNING AFTER A HALF-DOZEN MARTINIS.
WOULDN'T KNOW, VERONICA. I DON'T DRINK 'EM.
IT'S CAROL. AND WE NEED TO MOVE BEFORE THAT ROCK SPARKS BACK UP.
DON'T GET YOUR GRANDMA PANTIES IN A BUNCH.
FIRST THINGS FIRST.
YA SEEN MY HAT?
I AM

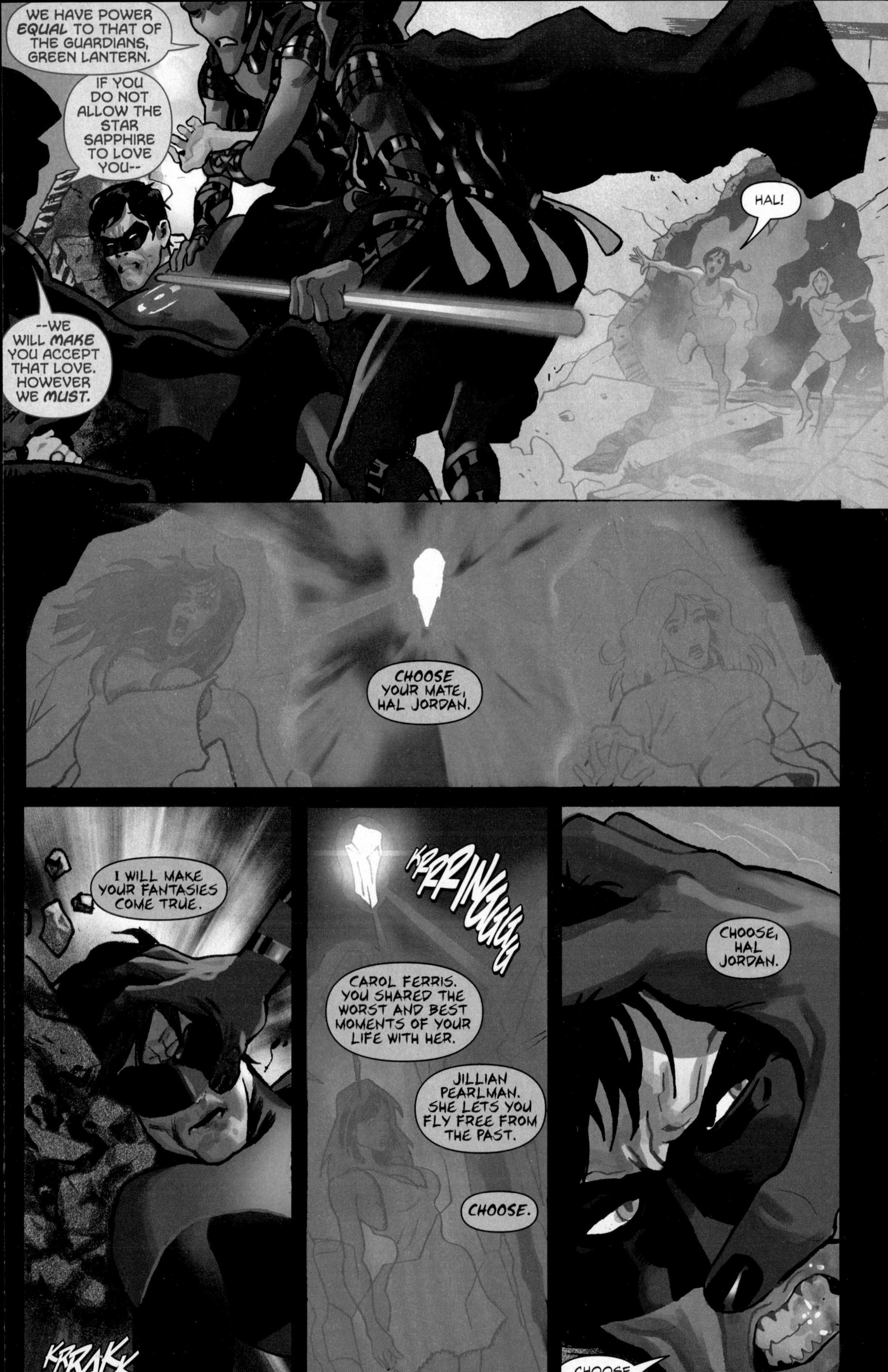
WE HAVE POWER EQUAL TO THAT OF THE GUARDIANS, GREEN LANTERN.
IF YOU DO NOT ALLOW THE STAR SAPPHIRE TO LOVE YOU--
--WE WILL MAKE YOU ACCEPT THAT LOVE. HOWEVER WE MUST.
HAL!
CHOOSE YOUR MATE, HAL JORDAN.
I WILL MAKE YOUR FANTASIES COME TRUE.
KRRAKK
KRRRINGGG
CAROL FERRIS. YOU SHARED THE WORST AND BEST MOMENTS OF YOUR LIFE WITH HER.
JILLIAN PEARLMAN. SHE LETS YOU FLY FREE FROM THE PAST.
CHOOSE.
CHOOSE, HAL JORDAN.
CHOOSE SOMEONE. OKAY.

C'MERE, GORGEOUS.
WHAT ARE YOU DOING, GUARDIAN DOG?
TRYING NOT TO THROW UP.
HE HAS CHOSEN NEITHER OF YOU.

HE HAS CHOSEN YOU, MY QUEEN.

SOMEONE OF GREAT POWER. POWER TO ADD TO MINE.

HONOR GUARDS, STOP IT--

AAAIEEE!

IT HAS BEEN SO LONG SINCE I HAD SUCH POWER.

SUCH LOVE.

<NO!>

<GET OFF OF HER!>

FZZZAK
<YOU STAND IN MY WAY, ZAMARON.>
<LOVE WILL CONQUER ALL.>
SO YOU THREW A LITTLE AFFECTION AT SOMEONE ELSE AND THE ROCK FELL FOR IT?
JEALOUS?
SKRAK
SKRAK
<LET GO!>
<THE SAPPHIRE IS GROWING AS POWERFUL AS OUR SISTER. IT IS ATTACHING ITSELF TO HER LIFE WEB.>
<WE NEED TO REMOVE IT, BUT WE DO NOT HAVE THE CAPABILITY TO DO THAT SAFELY HERE.>
<THEN WE TAKE HER HOME.>
FWASSSH
YOU DO NOT UNDERSTAND THE SCALES YOU ARE TIPPING OUT OF BALANCE, GREEN LANTERN.
THE NEXT REBIRTH IS UPON US ALL AND, THANKS TO YOU, EARTH IS NOW UNPROTECTED AGAINST IT.
YOU DON'T UNDERSTAND WHAT LOVE TRULY IS.
NOT THE FIRST TIME I'VE HEARD THAT.
SO... LADIES...
...WHO'S UP FOR A DRINK?

EDWARDS AIR FORCE BASE.
PANCHO'S.
WHAT CAN I GET YOU ALL?
BEER.
AND YOU, MA'AM?
MARTINI. DIRTY.
"DIRTY," MA'AM?
WITH OLIVE JUICE.
I'LL SEE WHAT WE CAN DO.
HEY, COWGIRL. YOU LEFT THIS HERE.
THANKS, SHARRY!

I TAKE IT YOU COME HERE A LOT?
BACK IN THE DAY, YOU WOULDN'T BE CAUGHT DEAD IN A PILOT BAR.
SO YOU TWO HAVE TANGLED A FEW TIMES, *huh?*
HAL AND I DATED ON AND OFF--
ACTUALLY, I WAS TALKIN' 'BOUT THE SAPPHIRE.
THE CORPS IS SENDING A BIOHAZARD UNIT TO ZAMARON TO FOLLOW UP. AND SALAAK IS ATTEMPTING TO GET THE GUARDIANS INVOLVED.
WHAT'S A SALAAK?
...*um*... I WOULDN'T WANT TO BORE YOU--
LISTEN, I SHOULD GET GOING ANYWAY.
THE RING GAVE YOU A CLEAN BILL OF HEALTH.
FIRST ROUND IS ON ME.
CAROL, WHY DON'T YOU--
IT WAS NICE MEETING YOU, JILL.

SOMETHIN' I SAID?
DON'T WORRY ABOUT IT.
I GUESS SHE'S MOVIN' ON.

WHAT ABOUT *YOU?*

WHAT ARE YOU DOING SATURDAY NIGHT?

WHATEVER YA GOT IN MIND, SUPER-HERO.

ZAMARON.

<PERHAPS THE EARTHMAN WAS CORRECT. THE POWER THE SAPPHIRE HOLDS OVER ITS HOST IS OVERWHELMING.>
<AND UNABLE TO BE REASONED WITH.>
KRRAKKK

<THE FARTHER AWAY FROM THE CENTER OF THE EMOTIONAL SPECTRUM, THE GREATER THE INFLUENCE OVER THE BEARER.>

KRRRKSHH
<THEN WE RECTIFY THAT.>

<AND WE TAKE A PAGE FROM THE BOOK OF OA.>

<WE HAVE BEEN OBSESSED WITH THE STUDY OF THIS ONE EMOTION FOR SO LONG, WE HAVE DONE WHAT THE GUARDIANS HAVE.>
<WE ABANDONED EMOTIONS.>
<WE CAN TURN AWAY FROM THE OTHERS NO LONGER.>
<IT IS TIME TO NOT ONLY COLLECT *LOVE*...>
<...BUT TO COMBAT THE PROPHECY...>
FWASHH

<...WE MUST COLLECT THEM ALL.>

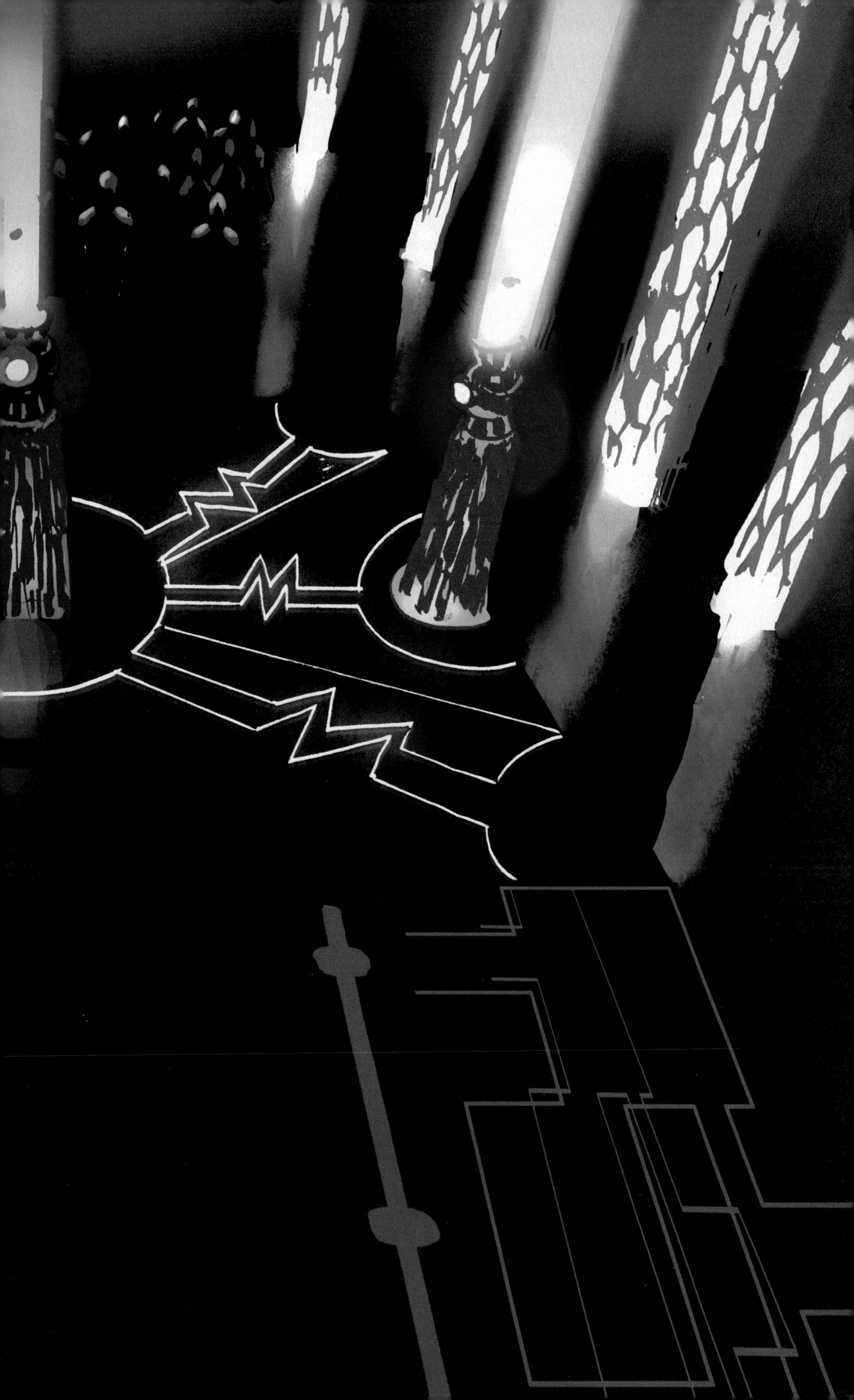

SOUTHERN CALIFORNIA.
FERRIS AIR.
...CAROL'S NEW PARTNER AND YOU'RE STILL TAKING ENGINES APART?
I'M NEVER GONNA STOP WALKING AROUND WITH A WRENCH. IT'S *MY POWER RING.*
I SWUNG BY TO SAY *CONGRATULATIONS,* TOM.
AND TO CHECK IN ON CAROL.
WANTED TO MAKE SURE SHE WASN'T TOO RATTLED ABOUT YESTERDAY.
CAROL FERRIS DOESN'T *GET* RATTLED, HAL.
SHE'S BACK IN THE AIR. WORKING IT OUT HER OWN WAY.
SHE'S HAD A HARD YEAR. GETTING THE COMPANY UP AND RUNNING AGAIN. WORRYING ABOUT YOU WHEN *YOU* GOT BACK FROM RUSSIA.
...BUT I GOTTA TELL YA--
--SHE'S BEEN SMILIN' A LOT MORE SINCE THE DIVORCE.
DIVORCE?
END

BIOGRAPHIES

GEOFF JOHNS got his first break in comics writing STARS AND S.T.R.I.P.E., which he created for DC Comics. He has since become one of the most prolific and popular writers in the industry, having worked on such titles as THE FLASH, TEEN TITANS, HAWKMAN, 52, INFINITE CRISIS and JUSTICE SOCIETY OF AMERICA. He is reunited with his mentor, Richard Donner, as they co-write ACTION COMICS.

IVAN REIS is a Brazilian comic book artist who began working for Dark Horse Comics on such titles as *Ghost, The Mask* and *Xena*. For Marvel, he has worked on *Iron Man, Captain Marvel* and *The Avengers*. His DC work includes ACTION COMICS, RANN-THANAGAR WAR and, of course, GREEN LANTERN.

DANIEL ACUÑA lives in a little village in Murcia, Spain. He first became known to American comic readers for his striking covers on such DC titles as THE OUTSIDERS, JLA, THE FLASH, CRISIS AFTERMATH: BATTLE FOR BLÜDHAVEN as well as Marvel's *Captain Universe* and *Doc Samson*. After finishing his first project as full interior artist — pencils, inks and colors — on an American comic, the 8-issue miniseries UNCLE SAM AND THE FREEDOM FIGHTERS, he moved on to bring his talents to the GREEN LANTERN tales collected in this volume.

OCLAIR ALBERT grew up in the sixties reading and loving super-hero comics. His passion for the medium was so great he decided he had to work in the field and started inking professionally in the early nineties. During his career, he's worked on such titles as *Xena*, *Lady Death*, *The Vision* and *The Avengers*. For DC Comics, Oclair has inked issues of ACTION COMICS, SUPERMAN, INFINITE CRISIS and recently joined Ivan Reis on GREEN LANTERN.